THE
COLOR
SCHEME
BIBLE

THE

COLOR
SCHEME
BIBLE

Inspirational palettes for
designing home interiors

Anna Starmer

FIREFLY BOOKS

A FIREFLY BOOK

Published by Firefly Books Ltd. 2012

Fifth printing, 2017

Publisher Cataloging-in-Publication Data (U.S.)

Starmer, Anna.
    The color scheme bible : inspirational palettes for
designing home interiors / Anna Starmer.
[256] p. : col. ill. ;   cm.
Includes index.
Summary: A guide to using color in the home, describing
how colors interact and the effects they have on a room. 150
color schemes included.
ISBN-13: 978-1-77085-093-4 (pbk.)
1. Color in interior decoration. 2. Color guides. I. Title.
747/.94 dc23   NK2115.5.C6S837   2012

**Library and Archives Canada Cataloguing
in Publication**

Starmer, Anna
    The color scheme bible : inspirational palettes for
designing home interiors / Anna Starmer.
Includes index.
ISBN-13: 978-1-77085-093-4
1. Color in interior decoration. I. Title.
NK2115.5.C6S72 2012   747/.94 C2012-904035-5

Published in the United States by
Firefly Books (U.S.) Inc.
P.O. Box 1338, Ellicott Station
Buffalo, New York 14205

Published in Canada by
Firefly Books Ltd.
50 Staples Avenue, Unit 1
Richmond Hill, Ontario L4B 0A7

Manufactured in Singapore by Chroma Graphics
Printed in China by 1010 Printing International Ltd.

Conceived, designed, and produced by
Quarto Publishing plc
The Old Brewery
6 Blundell Street
London N7 9BH

QUAR.CSB2

Art Editor Anna Knight, Stephen Minns
Designer Louise Clements, Karin Skanberg
Project Editor Trisha Telep
Picture Researcher Claudia Tate
Assistant Art Director Penny Cobb
Art Director Moira Clinch
Publisher Piers Spence

Contents

How to use *this book*

This book contains 200 inspirational color palettes for home decorators and interior designers. The text accompanying each palette discusses the moods the colors evoke, and will help you create your desired ambience. There is also practical application guidance, which will help you approach the room as a whole, and advice on the kind of finishing touches that suit the particular scheme.

At the beginning of the book you will find information on color theory, along with some ideas on how to create your own schemes and designs. While it is helpful to have some basic understanding of color theory and principles, it is also important to create a room that you, your family and your friends are going to enjoy. You can also use the world around you as a source of inspiration, gathering tips and ideas from everyday life, and learning to really enjoy color.

To help you make your own color choices at home, the book is separated into nine color chapters: Pinks, Reds, Oranges and Browns, Yellows, Greens, Blues, Violets, Neutrals and Grays. Each chapter contains many levels and tones of color, from bright, pure primaries through to delicate, tinted pales. We have chosen some classic color combinations with an almost timeless quality, as well as contemporary schemes that can bring a fresh look to any style of house.

Using the palettes

(1) Color-coded bullets correspond to the color chapter that you are in.

(2) Mood-enhancing words to help you imagine the feeling each scheme will evoke.

(3) The inspiration behind the color choices. This section tells you about the main color for the room.

(4) This is the theory behind the interior-design style. Find ideas and inspiration on materials and finishes, flooring, furniture, pattern and accessories.

(5) The main color in the room, to be used on all, or most of, the wall space. Take this book to your local paint store and ask them to match a test pot to this color. Paint a square of color on your chosen wall and let it dry, paint always changes color when it dries. Live with the color for a day or two to see if you really do love it before committing to a whole room.

(6) Alongside the main hue, are slightly differing tones of the same

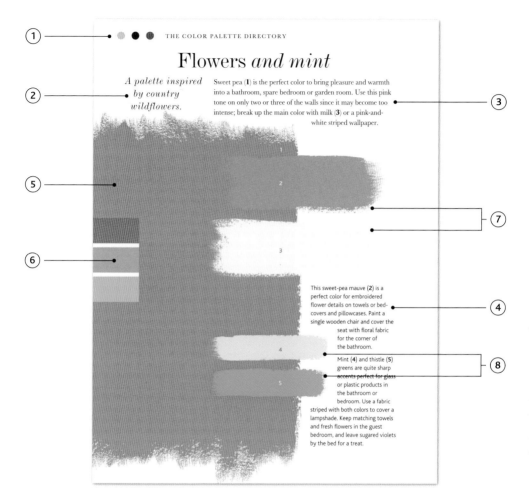

①

THE COLOR PALETTE DIRECTORY

Flowers *and mint*

②

A palette inspired by country wildflowers.

Sweet pea (**1**) is the perfect color to bring pleasure and warmth into a bathroom, spare bedroom or garden room. Use this pink tone on only two or three of the walls since it may become too intense; break up the main color with milk (**3**) or a pink-and-white striped wallpaper.

③

⑤

⑦

⑥

This sweet-pea mauve (**2**) is a perfect color for embroidered flower details on towels or bed-covers and pillowcases. Paint a single wooden chair and cover the seat with floral fabric for the corner of the bathroom.

④

Mint (**4**) and thistle (**5**) greens are quite sharp accents perfect for glass or plastic products in the bathroom or bedroom. Use a fabric striped with both colors to cover a lampshade. Keep matching towels and fresh flowers in the guest bedroom, and leave sugared violets by the bed for a treat.

⑧

---

color. If you are not entirely happy with the main color, this is the place to look for an alternative.

⑦ The accent colors can be used for an adjacent wall, for woodwork or to match to upholstery fabrics. The colors may be darker or lighter tones of the main shade, neutral shades to balance a room or complementary colors that create a contrast in an interior.

⑧ Each scheme also features two highlight colors. These can take the form of a sharp injection of color against a pale wall, such as a red glass vase in a pale blue interior, or the final balancing tone in a range of harmonious colors, such as deep chocolate brown in a room of luxurious coffee tones. The highlight colors, although only used in small quantities, are often the most important shades of all because they really complete the design.

Color in the home

A house is much more than just a roof over our heads. Our places of dwelling have developed dramatically over the course of history. Homes today have to be incredibly versatile buildings, often serving as a restaurant, kindergarten, hotel, office, library and sanctuary. The places in which we live should be enjoyed, provide protection, respite, peace, inspiration and warmth to all who enter.

Mix modern with traditional: use contrasting elements such as pale aqua with a highlight of bold neon orange, or ornate French furniture with soft metallics and bright, shiny acrylic plastic.

Color can dramatically alter any space within a home. The possibilities made available to us by modern paints are almost limitless, and traditional and modern homes alike can be transformed through the clever use of color. Pale colors and whites can instantly refresh a tired room, giving a clean look and creating a bright, spacious atmosphere. Rich colors, such as deep ruby or emerald green, will have an intense effect, creating a more intimate and cozy feeling.

Color in the home cannot be changed as often as we change our clothing, so the color decision is extremely important. This book aims to help you choose that all-important scheme, and to ensure that the choice suits your lifestyle and meets your personal and emotional needs.

Color for today

Color is one of the most exciting raw materials on earth. Since the beginning of time people have been using color to mark territory and decorate their surroundings. Color is powerful – it can cleanse and revive a tired area in any home, and can change a mood and lift the spirits. Across the globe different cultures attach significance to certain colors. Color can be passionate and sensual, and it can be calming and meditative.

Colors make an impression on all of us, and color and texture help to make our world a fascinating and beautiful place to live. Yet color is a reasonably modern luxury. Only 100 years ago color was the preserve of the wealthy, and there was no color television, no glossy color magazines or books, no plastics and limited textile dyes. For the majority, the world was many shades of gray.

However, in the 1950s the chemical industry made it possible to produce many more colors in dye and paint. It is possible today to create over 16 million separate colors. Developments in paint technology have also meant that we can now buy thousands of different paint types, ranging from basic latex paints through to metallic finishes, eco-friendly natural paints and even magnetic paint.

Color with confidence

Using paint is a simple and cost-effective way to completely restore and revive any area in the home. Never before has there been such a wide choice of color in paints, wallpapers, furniture and fabrics, allowing us to make our own designs and statements with color. But with so much choice, where do we begin? With all these possibilities, making color choices for the home can confuse and intimidate both the amateur and professional decorator. Many paint manufacturers boast that they can match almost any color, which is an incredible resource. But how can we decide on that perfect shade?

Enliven a tired guest room. Lavender is warmed up with fiery orange and bright magenta highlights. A bold use of pattern is a truly confident way to finish this welcoming guest interior.

This book can help you choose the right color for you, your room and its situation, and then show you how to build a stunning interior design around that color. Choosing the correct scheme for a room can transform a space from a tired living area into a stylish one. The right decisions made early on can have dramatic effects, which will not only impress your friends and family, but could even add value to your property. This book will arm you with the theoretical knowledge, a little inspiration and a conviction in your own tastes that in turn will give you the confidence you need to use color to its full potential.

SPEAKING PRACTICALLY

There are many factors to consider before you begin the work of filling a space with color. A small amount of practical knowledge and creative inspiration can go a long way in helping you to make the right choices. When choosing colors for your home, ask yourself some of these questions:

- What is the room to be used for?
- Who uses the room the most?
- What time of day will the room be used the most?
- How much natural light does the room receive?
- What important architectural features are there in the room?
- Which large pieces of furniture are, or will be, in the room?
- Which colors are featured in the rooms directly adjacent to the room?
- What feelings and emotions do you want the room to convey?

Write down your answers to these questions and keep them in mind as you peruse the information and visual references in this book. You will soon hit upon the perfect color scheme for your room.

Deciphering the Rainbow

The way in which each of us views color is unique. Our vision is tremendously complex and sensitive. Many external factors, such as lighting, adjacent color and surface texture, influence how we see color. There are several differing schools of thought surrounding color theory. In this book we will stick to some simple color principles, which can help you to successfully mix color, surfaces and objects within a room. A basic understanding of color theory will help you in your choice of colors. If you have some knowledge of the natural harmonies and discords between colors, creating your own color schemes becomes much easier. Master these simple principles and you will be able to mix colors with confidence.

A harmonious palette of oranges and golds. A soft pumpkin wall color is enhanced by complementary accents from one color family.

Color *theory*

Color is taken for granted today as an intrinsic part of every waking moment. It is beneficial, however, to make a point to learn how the human eye perceives color. The following scientific principles can be used as much or as little as you like. They can help you to make decorating decisions that will turn a simple color scheme into a successful interior.

Isaac Newton (1642–1727) explained that color originates in light. After much experimentation he worked out that light is made up of several different colors, and when he refracted light through a prism he was presented with the seven colors of the rainbow: red, orange, yellow, green, cyan (light blue), indigo (dark blue) and violet. Newtonian principles are still used today.

Thomas Young (1773–1829) took Newton's studies one step further when he realized that just three of the colors in the rainbow make up white light: red, green and blue. These three colors are the original primary colors. In 1859 the German physiologist Herman Von Helmholtz (1821–1894) built on Young's work and developed the theory that our eyes read color in terms of light, in red, green and blue. This theory was widely accepted and showed that every object is "coded" or broken down by the brain into various percentages of red, green and blue, which is how we see color.

Hering's color wheel

On this wheel, yellow is the fourth "primary" color. Ewald Hering (1834–1918) opposed the teachings of Helmholtz, believing that his chart gave a truer indication of the human experience of color. He argued that yellow ought to be a primary color because it is seen by the eye as an independent color, along with

All surfaces absorb and reflect light, breaking it down into separate colors. The human eye can only see the colors which are reflected. This is how we visualize color.

Green   Black   White

This diagram shows a four-color primary wheel, developed in 1878 by a German physiologist, Ewald Hering.

red, green and blue. He also included black and white as basic visual primary colors. Hering described his order of colors as "the natural system of color sensations." Today his system forms the basis of the N.C.S., the Natural Color System, which is used all over the world as a color-matching tool.

HARMONIOUS COLORS

The four "primary" colors are red, blue, green and yellow. When these pure colors are mixed, the secondary colors of purple, turquoise, orange and lime are produced. As you move around the wheel you can immediately see the harmonies between the colors that are adjacent to each other. For instance, a palette made up of tones of yellow, lemon, marigold and terra-cotta will always be successful. These colors all originate from between yellow and orange on the color wheel and they have an intrinsic harmony with each other.

COMPLEMENTARY COLORS

Colors that sit opposite each other on the color wheel are called "complementary." These are opposing colors that vibrate against each other, or clash. Often you will not see complementary colors together in a scheme, but sometimes the clever use of a complementary color in a room can have a striking effect. For instance, a bright turquoise chair against a soft orange-peach wall would look wonderful.

Colors to suit *you*

A little knowledge can go a long way, but rules are made to be broken. We can all be influenced by scientific theory and the current trends, but just remember the most important thing: it is you and your family who have to live with and enjoy these colors.

Use colors and pattern to really suit you, even if they are a little unusual or eccentric.

Never forget your own personal preferences and inspirations. If you simply love rich, jewel-like shades, then be bold and go for a luscious raspberry to inspire you in your work area. You can use your knowledge of the color wheel to perfect the actual shades and intensity of the colors, but do not be afraid to go with exactly what you love.

Simple color rules

Color began to be more widely available in home interiors after World War II. Particularly in Europe, after years of rationing during the war, color in the home seemed like a real luxury. During this period, a set of rules evolved, stating which colors worked best together. These are a good basis upon which to build ideas, but with so many more paint colors, application techniques and surfaces available to us today, we can easily go beyond these basic principles.

◀ All reds go together, as do all pinks. Certain shades of red and pink together can be great for a rich, passionate living room or a pastel, floral bedroom.

▶ Soft oranges are fantastically warming, and darker oranges must be used in moderation.

◀ Browns look great with orange. Turquoise and cool grays are good complementary colors to orange.

▶ Yellows go well with greens and oranges. Blues and yellows (complementary colors) create a classic interior combination for an upbeat, fresh environment.

◀ Green is often used like a neutral color to balance a room since certain shades of green, such as soft sage, can go with almost any other color.

▶ All blues go together and all greens go together. Shades of blue and green are fantastic together at all levels of intensity, from pale sky and duck egg through to dark inks and peacocks.

◀ Shades of violet can work well together, but may be too overpowering for most. Violets also look great with greens. Blue violets work well with cool blues, and red violets look beautiful with soft pinks.

▶ Grays and neutrals mix together well for a classic backdrop of unobtrusive tones, and such "colorless" palettes have been popular in the past and continue to be used today. Almost any color can be mixed with neutrals and grays to create unusual and stunning interiors.

Color and Mood

Every room in a house has the ability to evoke a mood and an atmosphere. A soft green bathroom can be a relaxing, calming environment, while a bright yellow entrance hall is warming and uplifting. Color, light and texture can stimulate the senses and awaken our emotions. Our homes can become a haven of mood-enhancing spaces to calm the soul and refresh the mind.

One of the most important aspects of decorating is creating the right kind of mood for you, an environment where you can be relaxed, comfortable, happy and content. If you are clever with paint, fabrics and lighting, you can dramatically alter the mood of a room and create a space tailor-made to your own lifestyle and emotional needs.

An elegant use of soft greens. Simple, yet pretty accents in pinks and pale blues help to create a calming, meditative mood.

Looking at *light*

Most of us do not usually consider the effects of light when decorating our home. Yet light can be the single most important element in making a scheme work. Living so much of our lives in artificial light, we often forget about the effects of changing light throughout the day, and how the passing of the seasons affects the way we see color.

Light coming in

Natural light keeps the world alive and you should take full advantage of it. Try to maximize the amount of daylight in your home with as many windows and skylights as possible. Make the most of strong summer sunlight by using the lightest, most diaphanous drapes at the windows in a bedroom or kitchen, which will let the wonderful light flood in. If an entrance seems very dark, consider a frosted glass door, which will let a diffused light through. Alternatively, use a block of bold color, such as geranium pink, on a single wall to lift the atmosphere of the area. It is often impossible to change the architectural details of a room, but clever use of color and light can easily make the most of any dark area in your home.

Make the most of natural light with large windows, glass paneled doors and pale colors on all the walls.

When deciding on a color scheme for a particular room, you need to consider the natural light that enters into it. Find out how strong the daylight is and spend some time in the room at different times of day, taking note of how the light affects it. For instance, if a room is facing northeast in the northern hemisphere, it will receive the least amount of natural light, so always use warming colors in this room to soften the shadows. If a bathroom has a large window and receives lots of natural light for most of the day, then a palette of cool blues and violets would look pretty, not cold.

Remember that at different times of the year, a room can take on different personalities. Just as the garden dies off in the fall, so too does the house become darker, curtains are closed earlier and more artificial lighting is used. You may wish to choose a scheme that works as well in daylight as in artificial light, such as warm mauves or coffee colors. Create a more cozy look in the dark winter months by simply changing bedspreads and cushions from crisp cotton to brushed flannels, velvets or fake fur. Place rugs or sheepskins on any bare flooring and drape soft, richly colored blankets on the backs of chairs and sofas.

Create a cozy atmosphere in a dark area with the use of soft lighting, and warming colors like reds and oranges.

Mood-creating light

Artificial light is a necessary part of our lives. Today there are many types of lighting available, and it is a good idea to consider alternatives to overhead lighting since it can be unflattering and harsh. Think about the activity that will take place in the room, and direct the light accordingly.

There are three main areas of lighting to consider. The first is task lighting, which is good, strong light used for working, cooking or reading. To achieve this, use daylight bulbs for a clearer view, and adjustable or telescopic lamps to direct the light. The second is ambient lighting, which is the general lighting in a room. It is often too bright, so choose low-level lighting or wall lights for a softer feel, and install a dimmer switch. Lastly, mood lighting is used to create a certain atmosphere, often a soft, romantic or intimate light. It should be kept at a low level – candles are perfect for creating a cozy, gentle mood.

Task lighting (below): Directional lighting aids specific needs, such as reading or preparing food.

Mood lighting (right): Low level, atmospheric lighting is perfect for quiet evenings at home.

Color and *emotions*

We are all emotional creatures and the modern world constantly inspires emotions within us. Being in a forest can make you feel peaceful, while sitting in a bright yellow café can make you feel stimulated or happy. However, often we are not aware of the effects the visual world has on our senses and our feelings.

A bold use of blues is exciting and inspiring. A suprise accent color lifts the spirit of any interior.

Certain colors can evoke a strong emotional response, and clever use of light can enhance or subdue a mood. So before you decorate, take the time to first consider how you want to feel in the room, and spend some time there before you decide on the final palette. Paint some test colors on the walls and observe how they change from day to night, and drape some fabric over a chair in front of the painted wall to see how the two colors and surfaces react with each other.

For example, in a home office that benefits from lots of natural daylight, you may wish to use a cool sky blue as the main color in order to stimulate clear thinking and a peaceful atmosphere. Yellow is a great color to use in a kitchen, and creates a citrus-fresh wake-up, or if a warmer tone is used, a cozy family space. If you decide on a passionate, hot-blooded scheme of red tones for the living room, then consider surfaces and fabrics that will enhance this sensual mood. Choose a high-gloss lipstick color for the woodwork and sumptuous velvets and smooth satins for the upholstery. Low-level candlelight is sure to finish this mood off perfectly.

Mood enhancers

Certain color groups will often inspire particular emotions. There are several emotions which certain color groups have been recognized as inspiring. These emotions can be altered dramatically depending on the depth or tone of the color, but the basic principles are worth remembering when deciding on your color palette.

Pinks are fun, lively, positive and feminine.

Reds are passionate, daring, intimate and comforting.

Oranges stimulate creativity and are warming and cozy.

Yellows are welcoming and sunny. Strong yellows are said
to help the brain work better.

Greens represent nature and are both tranquil and invigorating, as well
as restful and balancing.

Blues are connected to the sky and to water, and they are associated
with clear thinking and calm, meditative environments.

Violets can be stimulating and sexy, while blue violets can be cooling and spiritual.

Finding Inspiration

WHETHER YOU LIVE IN A CITY OR IN THE COUNTRY, THERE IS PLENTY TO INSPIRE. SIMPLY TAKE A LITTLE EXTRA TIME TO STOP AND LOOK AROUND. CONSIDER THE COLOR COMBINATIONS USED BY ADVERTISERS, SUCH AS ON BILLBOARD POSTERS OR FOOD PACKAGING. THESE COLORS HAVE BEEN CAREFULLY MATCHED BY GRAPHIC DESIGNERS, SO IT IS NO ACCIDENT THAT THEY LOOK GOOD TOGETHER. REMEMBER THE COLORS ON THE WALLS OF YOUR FAVORITE RESTAURANT. COLLECT FALLEN LEAVES TO INSPIRE A PALETTE OF RICH ORANGES AND OCHERS. LOOK CLOSELY AT THE MANY TONES IN A MENACING GRAY, STORMY SKY AGAINST THE WARM BROWN BARK OF A TREE. VISIT AN ART GALLERY AND LOOK CLOSELY AT THE TONES AND SHADES USED BY CLASSICAL AND CONTEMPORARY ARTISTS. YOU CAN FIND INSPIRATION ANYWHERE IF YOU TAKE A FEW MOMENTS TO SEEK IT OUT.

Take inspiration from the world around you. These weathered boats could be translated into a fantastic kitchen filled with green-and-blue-painted wooden cupboards.

Using *color scrapbooks*

Start carrying a small notebook around with you, and even a mini camera to keep track of your color observations. Collect bus tickets, candy wrappers, magazine pages, restaurant cards and flyers, and stick them in your book.

A rich, vibrant color scrapbook featuring your favorite items is the perfect base on which to build a great color library.

Take note of how colors you see make you feel, like how a field of bright red poppies can put a smile on your face, or how a woman's purple scarf against a gray sky can make you feel melancholy. Collecting colors is a fantastic game — suddenly your world becomes a huge painter's palette of inspiration and choice, and even the daily commute to work can become fun and interesting.

How to make a *mood board*

Mood boards are creative tools used by most designers, from fashion to interiors. A mood board is a visual story that is used to inspire a design team, or to explain to a client a certain design concept.

An inspirational collection of items to help in choosing specific colors, patterns and combinations.

Mood boards can be created from almost anything. They should be a considered representation of your research and taste. Look at the objects, photographs, cuttings, paint chips, fabrics and wallpaper swatches that you have collected. A favorite color scheme and style will begin to emerge. Once the mood board is finalized, use it as a constant reference throughout the decorating process.

Method

On a large board, lay out the reference materials you have gathered and consider how they look together. Play with scale, proportion and color on the board and try to find a harmonious combination. To do this, you can enlarge or reduce the size of specific items by using a color photocopier. Consider the colors that will be used most prominently in the room, for walls and floors for example, and try to display smaller pieces against these backdrop colors. Now try to visualize the proportion of color and pattern in your chosen room. This may take some imagination, so take the mood board into the room to help. Professional interior designers will often include a sketch of the intended final layout on a mood board to help the client visualize the end result. Try it for yourself.

A professional mood board of glossy images, colors, textures and fabrics was created as inspiration for the interior on the facing page.

The finished interior

A beautifully harmonious, yet modern bedroom interior was created from the information gathered in the mood board.

It is worth taking the time to learn a little about color, light and texture, and to learn which colors you personally love, before you start to decorate any area in the home. The mood board should be a considered conclusion to all of your research, and the final room will be a perfect interpretation of the mood that you have envisioned. The softened mauve of this room is dusty and flat, creating a perfect backdrop upon which to use rich color and bold textures. Soft mauve looks delicious with deep chocolates, although a bold highlight is needed to lift the colours and add a modern edge. The geranium-pink silk cushion adds a touch of glamor to the dark, quilted bedcovers, and the pink pattern contrasts well with the understated texture of the chocolate velvet bedspread. The bright magenta vase and pink flowers pick up the highlight color once again in polished glass, which catches the light perfectly. Different surfaces – from hard mirror and glass to soft velvets and silks – play with the diffused light in the room.

The Color Palette Directory

THIS EASY-TO-USE CHART ILLUSTRATES THE MAIN COLORS IN THE 200 PALETTES. AT A GLANCE YOU CAN SELECT A COLOR, THEN TURN TO THE CORRECT PAGE AND DISCOVER HOW TO USE IT EFFECTIVELY IN A PARTICULAR ROOM SCHEME.

38	39	40	41	42
43	44	45	46	47
48	49	50	51	52
53	54	55	56	57
58	59	62	63	64
65	66	67	68	69
70	71	72	73	74

75	76	77	78	79
82	83	84	85	86
87	88	89	90	91
92	93	94	95	96
97	98	99	100	101
102	103	104	105	108
109	110	111	112	113
114	115	116	117	118
119	120	121	122	123
124	125	126	127	128
129	130	131	134	135

136	137	138	139	140
141	142	143	144	145
146	147	148	149	150
151	152	153	154	155
156	157	160	161	162
163	164	165	166	167
168	169	170	171	172
173	174	175	176	177
178	179	180	181	182
183	184	185	186	187
190	191	192	193	194

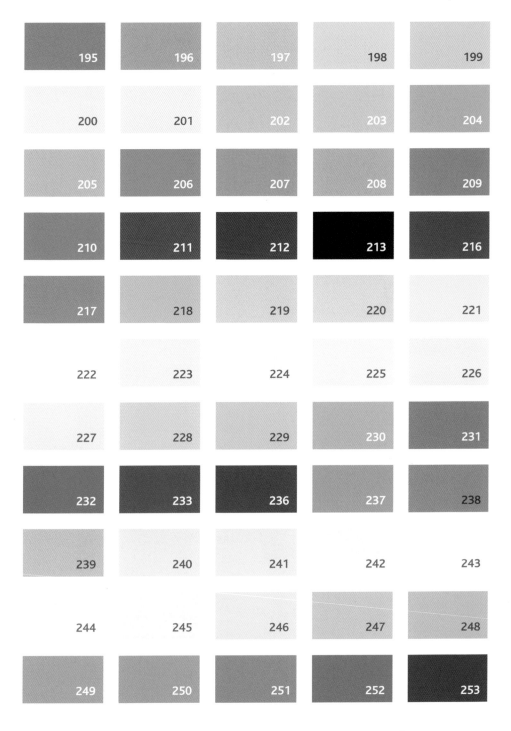

Pinks

Intense, *elegant and refined*

*A striking play
of dark and light
needs precise design.*

Cranberry (**1**) is contrasted with softened tones, a clever juxtaposition of colors that needs a precise, geometric plan to be successful. Dark colors draw in the room and need areas of light in order to prevent the atmosphere from becoming too somber. This truly modern palette evokes quality and good taste.

Tradition is knocked on the head here as darker tones are used for the walls and soft, delicate shades for the woodwork. Dusky pink (**2**) and soft stone (**3**) are classic interior colors and they add a touch of sensitivity to this strong, modern palette.

Sage green (**4**) balances the room with cool undertones, preventing the pinks from getting too pretty.

Black (**5**) has once again become very chic in interior design. Use on very glossy surfaces such as glass or lacquer. Try black serving plates in the dining room – they really complement the colors of food.

Raspberry *crushed velvet*

Rich and luscious raspberry (**1**) gives an instant feeling of sumptuousness. The highlight colors in this room are traditional interior colors from the turn of the last century. By combining such softened mid-tones with hot pink a truly contemporary interpretation is reached.

Soft, cozy vintage tones are fused with modern berry.

Warm and inviting, flat paints complement these dusted colors. Other surfaces in this room should be textural and tactile, like suede, knitted mohair or velvet.

Sueded buff (**2**) can be used for the flooring and larger pieces of furniture in the room, while mid-pink (**3**) is a perfect complement to the raspberry walls.

Accessorize in soft lavender (**4**) and smooth chocolate (**5**) for that added edge of grown-up sophistication.

This palette is perfect for a dining room or living area, where you will feel cozy, confident and creative.

Nostalgia *and naive memories*

Retro colors from the 1950s inspire a simple, easy palette.

This wonderfully intense magenta (**1**) is brought down to earth with a trip down memory lane. Look to old-fashioned children's storybook illustrations for color inspiration. A typically 1950s approach to using color can once again look new in this simple yet stylish design.

1

2

3

Use the darker cobalt (**3**) as the woodwork color and baby blue (**2**) for textiles. For curtains and cushions, mix the blues in stripes reminiscent of ship's deck-chairs.

4

5

Poppy (**4**) and snapdragon (**5**) can be used as accessory colors within the room for a real nostalgic touch. These pleasing sunset tones would work well as graphic imagery for the walls, or maybe for a fun tablecloth and napkins.

Spend time on the details in this room. Source vintage books and stack them on the mantelpiece to create a focus.

Fun *flamingo fantasy*

Bright flamingo (**1**) could work equally well in a fun room for children or a grown-up bedroom or dressing room. Such saturated colors can appear, at first, to be rather naive, but mixed with sophisticated shades of porcelain and orchid, a whole new environment emerges.

Pink breathes joy and cheer into any area of the home.

Tinted porcelain grays (**2**, **3**) are the perfect accent colors for bright pink. These cool, neutral tones almost soak up some of the intensity of pinks. Use for clean, linear surfaces, such as tinted glass tabletops or armoire doors.

Sweet orchid (**4**) and deep purple (**5**) should be used as the detail colors in patterned textiles.

Add quirky elements, such as purple glass knobs on an old chest of drawers, or paint some old terra-cotta pots and fill them with flowers.

Lively, *cheeky and playful*

A cheerful, enlivening palette is not just for children.

Rosy pink (**1**) works best when mixed with cooler colors, such as blue or blue-biased greens. This powerful combination of colors would look great in a modern, lively kitchen; choose pink laminate for the cupboard doors and source lots of fun, colorful accessories.

True aqua or turquoise (**2**) is a strong color to use anywhere in the home because it really draws in the eye. Use this in clever combination with a softer duck-egg blue (**3**) so that the mix of pink with blue does not become too harsh.

Lush, botanical lime greens (**4**, **5**) are fun accent colors. Source quirky plastic kitchen utensils, vibrant glazed ceramics and colored glass bowls in lime colors so that practical items can be left on show.

Mix all five of these colors to create a colorful mosaic of wall tiles for around the sink and oven.

Romantic, *delicate pearl*

Carnation (**1**) works very well when mixed with natural tones of shell and pearl. Such an intense main color in any room needs highlights that will soften the overall look. This is a great palette for a bedroom; accessorize with rose-tinted chandeliers, satin quilted throws and creamy, deep-pile carpets.

Heady pinks are perfect for a fragrant boudoir.

These accent colors are inspired by the soft, natural hues of giant seashells and mother-of-pearl. Try to find some accessories with shell or pearlized surfaces, such as coasters, jewelry boxes, small bowls or soap dishes. Vintage pieces can easily be found, but many modern outlets now produce good imitation pearlized trinkets.

For a special touch, mix pearlized glaze with delicate pink (**2**) and shell (**3**) for a shimmering paint surface.

Honey (**4**) and lichen (**5**) add some shadowy touches to this otherwise overly pretty palette.

Calm, *serene and tranquil*

Cool yet pretty colors are perfect for a modern bathroom.

This delightful lavender (**1**) is not too pretty and mixes well with modern hyacinth blue and fresh violet for an easy, striking palette. Consider the details in a bathroom; for example, invest in quality chrome fittings. Try bonded, colored rubber instead of tiling on walls and floors.

1

2

3

Blues have been proven to evoke a calming feeling within a room. Violet (**2**) and cool hyacinth blue (**3**) will bring a sense of serenity to this pretty pink room. Use these tones on all woodwork in the room, including a paneled bath surround and bathroom cabinet.

4

5

Orchid (**5**) offers a sexy accent, preventing the room from becoming too cold. Use this for towels and a luxuriously textured bath mat.

Ice blue (**4**) is a wonderfully delicate tone that helps to balance the intensity of all the other colors, so use it for the flooring and shower curtain.

Eclectic, *contemporary, quirky*

Cotton candy (**1**) does not always have to be used in girly designs. Be bold when using strong color combinations, such as pink with lemon and rose. Add a touch of the unexpected in the accent shades and see a very individual and modern environment unfold before your eyes.

A unique blend of natural and synthetic colors.

Use dusky rose (**2**) on woodwork and soft furnishings. Choose light-weight, translucent fabrics in buttery lemon (**3**) for delicate, sheer curtains.

Highlight colors are hugely important in this room, the sharper the color the better. See the room come to life when the accent colors of turquoise and peach (**4**, **5**) are given an injection of bright neon.

In order to further intensify the drama of this palette, choose materials such as glass or trans-parent plastic to enhance the accents, then direct light sources toward these objects.

Strawberry *chocolate fondant*

Sexy, strawberry pinks add a touch of indulgent glamor.

Strawberry mousse (**1**) could work equally well in a room with lots of natural daylight or in a romantic candlelit evening room, making it perfect for a bedroom. Accessorize with beaded cushions and floral tea-light holders. Let layers of rose-tinted muslin replace curtains or shades.

Rich, expensive chocolates with sweet strawberry centers inspire these combinations for woodwork and accent colors. Use milk chocolate (**2**) for luxury leather and suede seating. Bitter chocolate (**3**) is perfect for window frames and deep baseboards.

For the truly daring, try using hot pink in the living area of the home. On romantic evenings, light candles and mocha-scented incense, and wrap up in cozy, pink cashmere sofa throws.

Collect kitsch accessories in bright, tones of raspberry fondant (**4**) and Turkish candy (**5**) for fun.

Charming, *languid and pleasing*

This palette of colors is at once peaceful and invigorating. Baby pink (**1**) is a lively color to use in any interior. Combined with softened, lavender tones, a languid, relaxing atmosphere prevails. A sharp injection of bubble-gum pink offers a necessary boost of energy, which is so important in any modern room.

The perfect room for entertaining is energized with pink.

Baby pink (**1**), the main tone, matures when mixed with dusty plum (**2**) and powdery lavender (**3**) on woodwork. If a room painted entirely in pink seems too overpowering, try painting one wall or a recess area in one of these lowlight colors.

The final two accent colors in this room are opposite in terms of vibrancy and color level. Bubble gum (**5**) is perfect for amusing accessories, such as cocktail glasses or risqué illustrations framed on the wall. Soft brown (**4**) is, in contrast, timid and soothing, perfectly rounding off this amiable palette.

Orchid, *hyacinth and violet*

An aromatic palette of florals from heather to lavender.

A medley of floral tones invokes a lush spring-garden ambience, perfect for a bathroom or a very feminine bedroom. Orchid (**1**) is enlivened with tonal shades of lavender and violet. By using scented candles and floral fabrics, you can create a greenhouse environment.

Sometimes using tones of the same color is more interesting and has more impact than the use of contrasting shades. Strong colors can look less garish and much more designed when used in combination with paler tones of the same color.

Heather colors (**2**, **3**) complement the pink tones of the main color in the room. Use these for fine woodwork and soft chair covers.

Blue hyacinth shades (**4**, **5**) are heavier colors and must be used sparingly, but they offer real grounding to this flowery room.

Faded *antique porcelain*

Shell (**1**) is a delicate tint of pink that works well in a light and sunny living room or solarium. The combination of soft and powdered pinks, greens and mauves is inspired by faded, vintage fabrics and antique, beaded handbags. Fill the room with flea market and thrift store finds, like overstuffed armchairs.

A perfect room for lazy afternoons of reading.

The success of this palette lies in the delicacy of the colors and the flat, almost grayed-off nature of the accents. Bring anything more pretty into this room and you instantly lose the air of elegance.

Use velvets and faded, woven fabrics in soft sage greens (**2**, **3**) to cover a selection of mismatched vintage armchairs, and to paint woodwork, including window frames and external doors.

These two graceful tones of dusty mauve (**4**, **5**) are perfect with the pink and greens. Mix all these tones in faded, floral fabrics for cushions or for covering old books.

Sensational, *sensual*

Show-stopping color, where accessories are the star attractions.

Tinted pink porcelain (**1**) works so well in this room that it almost goes unnoticed. The perfect background color is never overpowering, but simply frames the room's highlights. Take inspiration from art galleries, choose spectacular centerpieces and work the design around them.

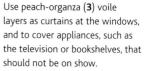

Use peach-organza (**3**) voile layers as curtains at the windows, and to cover appliances, such as the television or bookshelves, that should not be on show.

Muted peach melba (**2**) can be used for wood-work details and floors, but keep everything very sleek and simple.

Source items that you simply love in poppy (**5**) or Japanese lacquered red (**4**), such as an antique silk kimono hung above the fireplace or a single, heavy piece of Murano glassware. You could also make a multitude of small-scale scatter cushions in shantung or moire silk using these red colors.

Flawless, *laundered and pure*

Painting any room in the home white, or off-white, makes it feel instantly clean, light and new. Prettier tones of sun-bleached pastel, like blush (**1**), are perfect for a bedroom or bathroom. Accessorize with French monogrammed towels and embroidered bed linen. Place dried lavender in the laundry basket for a fresh smell to match.

A mix of immaculate, tinted whites for a spotless finish.

1

2

3

The main accent colors in this room are very cool and calming. Choose pale dove (**2**) to paint the woodwork, including the bedframe and headboard, as well as the floorboards.

Hint of blue (**3**) should be used for furniture within the room since this color is a happy partner to soft pink.

4

Dusky powder (**4**) and sunbeam (**5**) are the pretty elements in the room. Use in fine-striped linen to cover lampshades and cushions, or find oversized ceramic bowls to fill with soaps, silk flowers and shells.

5

Tuscan, *rustic and sun-kissed*

Sun-warmed tones are perfect for a country kitchen.

Tuscan pink (**1**) mixed with golden terra-cotta takes inspiration from the country houses of Tuscany in Italy, with their pale ochers and pasta yellows. These heirloom colors bring feelings of comfort into a kitchen. Accessorize with hand-thrown terra-cotta bowls filled with bread or lemons.

1

2

3

Use terra-cotta (**2**) for the floor tiles and work surfaces for a truly authentic, rustic look. Many hardware stores now stock real terra-cotta, or good imitation tiles, in a variety of shades.

Warm apricot (**3**) is the perfect country kitchen color, evocative of fresh jam and pretty wild-flowers. Use this color for curtains and cushions on kitchen chairs, and to paint the door that leads to the kitchen garden.

4

5

Use rich cream (**4**) for the ceiling to give an impression of extra light. A darker level of cream (**5**) is used for plates and milk jugs.

Garden party, *floral fancy*

Rose (**1**) is so pretty it should almost come perfumed. It completes an ambrosial palette perfect for a bedroom or well-loved living space. Make this room as flowery as you like, or keep the surfaces simple and let the colors work their magic.

Combine English florals with pretty, flower-hued pinks.

Ivory (**2**) is to be used on all woodwork. Use either matte or gloss finish, depending on how rustic a look you want.

Stone (**3**) is a greened neutral that can be used to paint large pieces of furniture, such as armoires and chests of drawers. This soft neutral works as a fantastic backdrop to the medley of pinks around the room.

Peony (**4**) and snapdragon (**5**) are taken directly from the garden, and they look as pretty in striped and floral textiles as they do in fresh cut flowers.

Decorative *baroque elegance*

A rich palette needing extensive ornamentation.

Antique pink (**1**) is the perfect backdrop for displaying gorgeous objects. Take a grandiose attitude toward home interior design and source baroque-style decorative furniture and large-scale replicas of 16th-century European art. This palette is perfect for a decadent bathroom or living room.

Pale gold (**3**) shimmers and shines on sensuous curved surfaces. Use it in the details, perhaps on picture or mirror frames, to catch the light.

Paint furniture in rich cream (**2**) and hand decorate the edges with gold. You could also source swirled door handles and candelabra in gold.

Use deep blackberry (**5**) for the flooring and choose deep-pile carpets or rugs.

Plush velvet in Venus red (**4**) can be used to cover chair seats. Pick out a few special accessories in this hot color, such as a glass vase or vintage perfume bottle.

Graphic, *urban and modern*

Coral (**1**) is taken in an unusually minimalist direction here. Neutral tones and cool teals are contrasting partners for a traditionally feminine color. This contemporary palette is perfect for open-plan living spaces, as blocks of color can be used in different areas, helping to segregate the environment.

Warm and cool tones in opposition inform an open-plan design.

Cement tones (**2**, **3**) can look fantastic when combined with vivid color. Take inspiration from modern retail environments, and opt for polished, tinted concrete for flooring and internal support pillars.

Dusty blue (**4**) could be used for large, free-standing pieces of furniture, such as a sofa or chaise longue.

Choose a strong color, such as teal (**5**), for kitchen surfaces. In an open-plan environment make a feature of the kitchen, rather than trying to conceal it with white.

Flowers *and mint*

A palette inspired by country wildflowers.

Sweet pea (**1**) is the perfect color to bring pleasure and warmth into a bathroom, spare bedroom or garden room. Use this pink tone on only two or three of the walls since it may become too intense; break up the main color with milk (**3**) or a pink-and-white striped wallpaper.

1

2

3

4

5

This sweet-pea mauve (**2**) is a perfect color for embroidered flower details on towels or bed-covers and pillowcases. Paint a single wooden chair and cover the seat with floral fabric for the corner of the bathroom.

Mint (**4**) and thistle (**5**) greens are quite sharp accents perfect for glass or plastic products in the bathroom or bedroom. Use a fabric striped with both colors to cover a lampshade. Keep matching towels and fresh flowers in the guest bedroom, and leave sugared violets by the bed for a treat.

Theatrical, *dramatic cabaret*

Delicious, voluptuous pink (**1**) creates an instantly glamorous and provocative environment. Use heavy drapes in this room and keep the lighting low, preferably with candleholders on the walls instead of electric lights. Raise the bed onto a platform for a touch of added drama.

A decadent bedroom inspired by the Moulin Rouge.

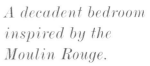

Glossy black (**2**) looks fabulous for window frames, baseboards and doors. Paint decorative mirror frames to match. Choose black, curled wrought ironwork for the curtain rod.

Use deep purple (**3**) in lengths of lace for a new take on net curtains, or to make a seductive bedspread.

Slate green (**4**) or dusty green (**5**) are perfect for slinky silk bedcovers.

Go to town with accessories in this room: fill vases with long feathers and cover the bed in beaded scatter cushions.

Simple *picnic fun*

A bright and lively palette for indoor family picnics.

This over-the-top palette using fuchsia (**1**) is great for a fun family room. Keep walls and furniture simple with clean lines, then use fun accessories to get just the right look. Existing furniture, such as chairs, kitchen cupboards and picture frames, can be painted in bright tones.

1

2

3

The sunny, pale yellows (**2**, **3**) are perfect for bringing the feeling of natural daylight into the home.

Accessories in this room can be as kitsch and playful as you like. Choose brightly colored plastics in sugar pink (**4**) and golden yellow (**5**) for plates and cutlery. These can be found with graphic floral or polka-dot prints.

4

5

Source a fun, striped, multicolored tablecloth to use as a picnic blanket. For a children's party make lots of colorful food, like pink and yellow cupcakes and pink lemonade.

Glowing, *radiant sunset*

Dense berry (**1**) needs luminous highlight colors to lift the room. Because this pink is so dark, it may make the room appear smaller – consider using pale peach (**3**) on one of the walls. Lighting is key here. You could even invest in a neon sign to hang on the wall.

Brilliant oranges complement this deep, crushed pink.

Pinky gray (**2**) will help to deflect the intensity of the other colors in the room. This elegant color can be used for carpet and luxury suede furniture.

Pale peach (**3**) is a beautiful color to use on woodwork in the room. Such a subtle hint of color contrasts well with the main, darker color.

Day-Glo peach (**4**) and sunset orange (**5**) can be used for colored-glass light fixtures and ornaments. Source graphic-patterned fabrics in these colors for cushions.

Reds

Classic *and characteristic*

A strict palette for a Japanese-inspired room.

Nothing about this interior is accidental – everything has a place or a function. The definitive shapes are linear and simple with strictly measured dimensions. Furniture is black lacquered wood and the inspiration is traditional Japanese. This deep, rich wine (**1**) is perfect for an intimate, stylized dining area.

This room needs little decoration; it is more about clean surfaces and lines.

Parchment (**3**) is perfect for simple paper lampshades, and paper sliding partition doors; if possible find wax-covered paper or handmade paper for an authentic look.

Gold (**5**) is a wonderfully vibrant color to use for chair cushions and small floor rugs.

Use a glossy, black lacquer (**2**) for high-backed chairs and a table, and red (**4**) for details, such as tassels and Japanese flowers.

Voluptuous *damson berry*

Port (**1**) comes from the blue-biased family of reds. When mixing with other red tones always marry from the same family, and stick to blue-biased or yellow-biased colors. Green is the opposing color on the color wheel, so it creates a dramatic contrast to red.

Sensuous, intense berry shades are not for the fainthearted.

Eggplant (**2**) is a wonderful, darker version of the main color, and it can be used on woodwork and flooring, either in carpets or dark, patina tiling.

Cyclamen (**3**) is also from the blue-biased family, so it works well in this scheme for furnishings. Cover a favorite old chair or sofa in cyclamen velvet for a practical yet fun focus in the room.

Chlorophyll (**4**) and brilliant turquoise (**5**) are opposite tones in this palette, creating a real vibrancy. Use these shocking hues for accessories, such as cushions, framed prints and fun glasses.

Earthy, *natural pigments*

Mineral colors inspired by real earth extracts.

The first paints ever made were from pigments, which are dyes taken from rock and earth colors. Ocher, sienna, umber and red earth (**1**) are natural colors that will give a restful feel to any environment. Natural paints are widely available so opt for toxin-free wall coatings.

Sand and stone (**2**, **3**) are very comfortable shades that can be used together for a discreet effect on woodwork and flooring, such as natural jute-woven matting. Using subtly different tones of the same color is a clever way to mimic nature. Subtlety can often be just as arresting as a stark contrast.

Iron ore (**4**) and deep sienna (**5**) are basic, fundamental colors that offer rich and endless possibilities. Use these tones in natural fabrics such as linen or hemp. Accessorize with stone, earthenware and dark woods.

Positive, *cheerful and carefree*

True crimson (**1**) is one of the primary colors. In its purest form it can fill a room with joy and laughter. For an informal environment, such as a family room, or a fun open-plan kitchen for entertaining, this palette is wonderfully naive and instantly pleasing. Use hard-wearing, practical surfaces in this room.

Lighthearted colors that simply make you smile.

Dawn blue (**2**) is used on woodwork as an alternative to white. This pale tint offers a cool antidote to the powerful crimson walls.

Bluebell (**3**) is a great color for plastics and other man-made materials. Choose ergonomically shaped seating and wipe-clean vinyl flooring.

Flame (**4**) and bright orange (**5**) are for cushions and utensils in the kitchen. Source playful plastic kitchen tools that children can use as easily as adults. Invest in a designer coat stand or a sleek, modern wall clock in resin or plastic.

Considered, *cool and careful*

A thoughtful use of contemplative colors for a study.

Muted but still vibrant, vermilion (**1**) has masculine undertones that need refined, classic colors to complement it. A grown-up combination of cool grays and neutral blues offers a balanced palette of modern contrasts. Grays are smart, luxurious interior shades.

1

2

3

Neutral tones can be cool or warm. Historically viewed as drab or dreary, such natural colors are now being celebrated for their relaxing, comforting charm.

Natural stone (**2**) and rain cloud (**3**) are perfect cooling colors for this red. Use them for wooden or woven flooring and comfy reading chairs.

4

5

In fashion, this deep charcoal (**4**) is seen as a perfect alternative to black. Use in this scheme for around the fireplace, on picture frames, and bookshelves – practical and stylish.

A flash of blue (**5**) is a highlight for cushions and desktop accessories.

Soft, *feminine and pretty*

A delightful arrangement of pretty pale accents lifts this dusty roseate (**1**) color. By opting for a softened or powdered red tone, the color is rich but not overpowering. Colors are softened, yet seductive, and surfaces are matte.

Mellow colors with an antique finish.

Myrtle green (**2**) can be used for large, soft furnishings in this bedroom or sitting room. Use soft fabrics and loose covers for chairs and side tables.

Coral (**3**) can be used as a stain or antique tint for woodwork, cupboards and armoires. Paint on one coat only and rub off excess paint to reveal some of the lovely natural wood beneath.

Pale peach (**4**) and panama hat (**5**) are perfect for decorative motifs and architectural features in the room. Use linen or 100 percent cotton with natural textures running through the fabrics.

Moroccan, *sumptuous and spicy*

An indulgent, heady room filled with extravagant scents.

Hot, sultry and flushed, red rose petal (**1**) creates a lavish backdrop to a room meant for hedonistic indulgence. Highly flavored and deeply decorated, this room is perfect for entertaining. Cover surfaces with candles in colorful Moroccan tea glasses.

Mulberry (**2**) is the secondary red tone in this room, further intensifying the grandeur. Use for traditional low seating, and mix with indigo and ruby silks from Morocco for scatter cushions and over-long window drapes.

Mahogany (**3**) is used for the wood furniture and woodwork in this room, such as low tables and a fireplace.

Purple accent colors (**4**, **5**) are great for patterned fabrics. Also source colored dishes and plates in which to serve the aromatic foods. Use colored-glass lanterns for a subdued lighting.

Stimulate, *revive and rejuvenate*

Modern coral (**1**) is enlivening and warming, great for a bath or shower room. Fresh and invigorating, this vibrating palette of reds and turquoises is a contrasting mix of brights. Even if every other room is calm and natural, go to town in a bathroom with colors that you simply love.

Dynamic colors are perfect for a wake-me-up bathroom.

Levels of bold turquoise blue (**2**, **3**) can be mixed together for tiling on the walls and floor – add a few random tiles in coral, too. Choose the paler of the two blues (**3**) for a plastic shower curtain and toilet-seat cover.

Violet (**4**) and neon pink (**5**) are modern highlights to be used sparingly and with a touch of humor. Source some kitsch, plastic accessories in these over-the-top shades.

Have a favorite phrase or mantra cut out in vinyl lettering to run around the walls of the room.

Shocking, *lively and confident*

A modern and bold palette, where neons work well with pales.

Shocking neon red (**1**) is a great color for a stairwell or dark area in your house; glowing undertones should be used in a hallway or area where people are moving around the house. Allow the color to vibrate and work – do not mix with other bright reds as this will deaden the impact.

Softened pink colors (**2**, **3**) perfectly ground the vibrant main shade, preventing the room from becoming too frivolous. In direct contrast, the pinks can be used for subtly toned ceilings, baseboards and picture frames. Cover an old, buttoned chair in soft pink silk for a brilliant clash of antique with contemporary.

Flashes of lemon lime and neon yellow (**4**, **5**) would be perfect for lamps and lights. Look for a dramatic, overscaled 1960s light as a focus on the landing.

Cherries, *blossoms*

A wonderful cherry (**1**) tinged with coral and pink could easily work in both a traditional or modern interior. For cozy, indulgent evenings and fresh sunny days, combine this flourishing red with a mixture of pale and full accent tones. This is a clever, natural palette of blushing pinks and bud greens.

Bright, cherry red is relaxed with spring blossom colors.

Delicate blossom (**2**) is used on the woodwork, window frames and ornate ceiling features in a room with traditional details.

Soft baize green (**3**) is to be used for furnishings, rugs and curtains. Source prints and landscape paintings incorporating these types of greens.

Deep moss (**4**) and rose (**5**) are natural tones to accessorize this room. Go as simplistic or decorative as you like.

Search through antique stores for decorative tiles for the fireplace. Pinks and greens are typical of the art nouveau period invoked here.

Unrefined *adobe clay*

An intuitive palette of unspoiled shades and natural finishes.

Natural terra-cotta (**1**) and adobe colors make a great kitchen palette. These warm shades invoke a cozy, family environment. Use natural stone on the floor and scrubbed, antique pine furniture. An open fireplace would be great as the focus of the room.

1

2

3

Sun-bleached bone (**2**) is a very pale color to be used in a family room, so use eggshell paint and waterproof fabric for chairs for a wipe-clean environment.

Pale pine (**3**) furniture is blocky and heavy for a lived-in quality.

4

5

Mud (**4**) and kidney bean (**5**) are lovely rustic shades, perfect for deep vegetable bowls, tiled work surfaces and your favorite leather chair by the fire.

These easygoing and relaxing colors are timeless. Invest in long-lasting furniture, and accessorize with new pictures and flowers when you feel like a change.

Jeweled, *precious scarlet*

Ruby, garnet (**1**), coral, jade, turquoise and emerald – this trinket box of opulent colors will enrich any room in the house. Experiment with new and different surface techniques, such as glazes and pearlized pigments, which further intensify the colors.

A treasure chest of rich colors needs no decoration.

These flame-colored tones (**2**, **3**) are similar, but work together to exaggerate the depth of color in this room. Use them together for glazed tabletops, cupboard doors or on a polished floor.

Pine-needle green (**5**) is a classic upholstery color, that could be brought up to date if used on modern furniture shapes.

Turquoise (**4**) is a wonderfully vibrant tone to use in shimmering fabrics for cushions and lamps with glass-beaded tassels.

For an unusual touch, create a feature on the wall with stick-on ruby rhinestones.

Fiery, *exotic and wild*

Flaming red walls are passionate and enticing.

The type of palette that could easily spill from inside out into the garden. Mix together shades of flame (**1**), pink and orange for the perfect summer party look. Imagine low seating, rugs, scatter cushions, sequined sari fabrics as curtains for patio doors and colored glass lanterns.

This environment could be a haven for curiosities collected on foreign travels. Mix colorful Indian silks with classic Indonesian batik fabrics for cushions and curtains. Hang wind chimes in the trees and burn *nag champa* incense.

Mix and match these intense shades in contrasting patterns, textures and surfaces. Source a traditional Indian pagoda or large sun umbrella in these deep reds and oranges (**2**, **3**), dark ebony wood for furniture and magenta (**4**, **5**) silk for cushions.

Plush, *fine and jet set*

Deep ruby (**1**) alludes to a luxurious and expensive interior. These colors cry out for quality surfaces, such as plush, deep-pile carpets, buckskin leathers, polished lacquer tabletops and red Venetian glassware. Create a classical and refined room with plenty of details.

A palette inspired by the private jets of the rich and famous.

This palette could decorate a grand entrance hall, a dining area or a swish dressing room with concealed doors and underlit mirrors. Everything in this interior is tailor-made. For an alternative wall or floor covering why not go for soft leather panels?

Light cream and soft nubuck (**2**, **3**) are for leather seating and woodwork, contrasting with the ruby walls.

Black cherry (**4**) and navy (**5**) complete this quality mix; use on ostrich leather footstools, hand-crafted door handles and elegant glass lighting.

Aristocratic *pastoral*

Traditional country estates inspire this high-class palette.

Academy red (**1**), racing green and hunting brown were once colors reserved for English royalty. But today we can all enjoy these traditional shades. With the long tradition of handmade furniture and country living, this is a palette that will stand the test of time.

1

2

3

Colors of the land, forest (**2**) and fern (**3**) are perfect for furnishings and curtains. Choose heavy fabrics to exaggerate the feeling of luxury.

Pine cone (**4**) and chestnut (**5**) can be used for rich carpets and expensive-looking wooden furniture.

4

5

This room should be accessorized with paintings of traditional hunt scenes or vast landscapes. Source leather-bound books for book-shelves and an old-fashioned writing desk with a leather chair.

Composed, *restful and settled*

This is an unusually relaxing rust (**1**) color scheme that is perfect for historic properties, since it maintains a standard of authenticity. But don't confine such a great color scheme to traditional environments. Take these natural tones into a modern living space and feel it become instantly cozy.

A dependable palette of rust red with rosy undertones.

This is a great palette for a kitchen or a dining or sitting room. The rich rust red background is an easy color to work with, accepting many natural hues quite easily.

Brick (**2**) and hen's egg (**3**) are equally reliable tones, perfect for interior and exterior woodwork and flooring in wood, tiles or vinyl.

Straw (**4**) is a great color for seating and curtains. In patterns or stripes, mix this color with white for a fresh touch.

Sunny yellow (**5**) adds a touch of brightness in plates and teacups displayed in a hutch or sideboard.

History, *heritage and heirlooms*

Spend time to reproduce a home's original style.

Make the most of the great variety of heritage paint colors on offer today, which instantly create an authentic atmosphere in a historic property. The naturally-aged colors of worn and loved textiles enhance any traditional room. Radicchio (**1**) is perfect for a study or living room.

1

2

3

The highlight colors in the room draw on historical reference, but are definitely not old-fashioned. Used cleverly and with more contemporary accessories and shapes, this palette can be brought up to date.

Rust (**2**) can be used for windows, photo frames and baseboards.

4

5

Ketchup (**3**) is a great color for contemporary, bold furniture.

Army green (**4**) and air-force blue (**5**), common colors of the 1940s, are once again the height of fashion. Use military fabrics to cover cushions for a quirky alternative textile.

Afternoon tea: *antique tradition*

Claret (**1**) is softened with warm colors of petal peach and chiffon orange. Mid-tones of pinky mink help this quirky palette to blend. This room should be decorative, with floral fabrics and vintage plates hung on the walls. Revive the tradition of afternoon tea for a fun party with friends.

Delicious, dark claret red with tea-stained tones.

Deep red needs delicate colors to soften it. Use pinky mink (**3**) and copper blush (**2**) on different facets of the woodwork, creating graded stripes of color. The warm, tinted neutral soaks up the rich red.

Use petal peach (**4**) and chiffon orange (**5**) for accessories. Source floral silk scarves to make into original, mismatched cushions. Use 1940s handbags, shoes, gloves or veiled hats to hang from picture frames and the mantelpiece.

Antique, floral porcelain tea sets are great to leave on the table. Fill with roses or old-fashioned candy.

Oranges
and Browns

Bitter chocolate, *sweet centers*

An irresistible blend of deep brown, mint, and sugared violet.

Dark chocolate (**1**) is rich, but with red undertones, making it incredibly warming and welcoming in a room. It is perfect for a private haven, far from the hustle and bustle of everyday life. Such deep colors create a cocoon-like environment where you can indulge yourself in your own world.

Sugared violet (**3**) is a wonderfully delicate and pretty color to use in conjunction with the sexy brown. Use this accent color on woodwork, including any features such as chair rails, baseboards and a ceiling rose.

Pansy (**2**) is a dusty mauve, perfect for soft furnishings and big, feather-padded sofas and armchairs.

Use mint (**4**) and jade (**5**) to cool the palette. For a modern edge, use green glass for shelving in alcoves, and source an elegant green glass chandelier. Use green tiling around the fire, and green glass candlesticks on the mantel.

Mahogany, *chestnut and teak*

A natural palette inspired by the rich coloration of highly polished wood. Mahogany (**1**) is a deep-red, wood color. Choose this tone for walls in an elaborate, unusual bedroom environment. Mix with redwood furniture and accessories, such as a heavy four-poster bed and deep-framed paintings on the walls.

Rich auburn tones look wonderful with ginger and lemon.

Choose oatmeal (**2**) for natural woodwork, closet doors and wooden shutters at the windows.

Buttercup (**3**) is a strong, vibrant color that adds a modern edge to this natural palette. Use this highlight color for covering chairs and for curtains that the sun can naturally filter through.

These two shades of ginger (**4**, **5**) are perfect for the bedcovers and accessories. Mix textures on a bed with soft, satin duvets and cozy, fake-fur pillows. Stack old leather books by the bed with a simple brass lamp.

Toasted, *warming and cozy*

A glowing, burnished palette perfect for a lively kitchen.

This shade of toast (**1**) is wonderfully warming. A traditional color is brought up to date when mixed with opulent purples and pinks. Suited to both traditional and modern environments, it's decadent on dark, winter evenings and luxurious in the summer months.

Such deep color is not often found in a kitchen, but this palette is sure to delight both chef and dinner guests alike. Go for melt-in-the-mouth surface colors inspired by your favorite dishes, such as caramel pudding or tiramisu.

Use dusty plum (**3**) as the woodwork color in this delicious room, a softened color that complements both the pinks and the browns. Blackberry (**2**) is a great color for kitchen cabinets.

Fuchsia (**4**) and coffee (**5**) can be used for accessories in the kitchen and matched to the soft furnishings.

Traditional, *historic folk shades*

A palette of natural pigments and dyes that have stood the test of time. Colors are created from the earth and fabrics are woven wool or animal skins. Spice (**1**) is a wonderfully earthy, fiery color to have in a living or dining area.

A palette of folkloric colors inspired by the spice route.

Sienna (**2**) is a great color for low, heavy furniture. Be influenced by the styles of Turkey with low seating and patterned rugs.

Henna (**3**) is a softened color that can be used for curtains and large cushions in the room. Choose natural wool, linen and hemp fabrics.

Sandstone (**4**) and ivory (**5**) can be mixed with the other colors in traditional paisley or Ikat, an extraordinary silk fabric woven throughout Asia, for rugs, throws and wall hangings.

Teasing, *amusing and uplifting*

A joyful range of soft and light colors for bed or bath.

Have fun when choosing the colors for your home. Design is often taken far too seriously, so be bold and adventurous in your color decision-making. Cinnamon punch (**1**) is a warming color that is lifted and enlightened with tones of pink, ripe berry and mandarin.

Bubble gum (**2**) and pale rose (**3**) can be used for the woodwork, curtains and bedcovers. Choose a floral fabric for a pretty look, or opt for a simple stripe or polka dot for something quirky. Use the paler pink to paint floorboards, or for vinyl or laminated flooring in a bathroom.

Fabrics with dots or stripes in very berry (**4**) can be used as accents in the room. Use this color to make small cushions for the bed.

Zingy mandarin (**5**) is a sharp accent that gives the whole room a lift. Use it on lampshades and drawer handles.

Persimmon: *ripe and fruity*

Persimmon (**1**) is a lush, orange-red fruit and a wonderful color for a bedroom or family area. Use this tone with other fruit and berry colors for a rich yet mellow environment. In contrast, tinted, neutral tones help to season the palette, naturally balancing the colors.

A glorious palette of ripe fruit colors and soft, tinted neutrals.

Pomegranate-seed red (**3**) is a jewel of a color – bright and glassy as the name suggests. Use this color for rich, leather seats and chairs, and elaborate glass vases or bowls filled with fruits and flowers.

Tinted gray (**2**) offers a great tone to soak up some of the juicy colors. Use this for woodwork and flooring, either a luxurious carpet or polished concrete.

Pink grapefruit (**4**) can be used for cushions and shades for the window. Flowers in soft tea rose (**5**) make for a pretty room accent.

Architectural *and monumental*

Striking colors for a sweeping staircase or a grand entrance.

Strong burned orange (**1**) can be an overpowering interior shade. Use this color in an area where there is a lot of space, like a hall or stairwell. These colors are perfect for modern open-plan or double-height interiors, where color can help to segregate sections of the space.

Steel (**2**) and dapple (**3**) are heavy grays that work well together. Use them in stripes with the burned orange for curtains and furniture. Choose coated metal for picture frames and bannisters for an urban touch.

Lava (**4**) is a brash and overstated splash of color to catch the eye. Use it in an open-plan area to color a single piece of furniture. Alternatively, use it for the front door of the house, inside and out.

Cool blue (**5**) can be used for cupboard doors or as a painted square on the ceiling.

Bold, *powerful and melodramatic*

This is a fun combination of colors for a family bathroom. Red and orange traditionally clash, but the shades used here are similar enough to work together as highlights. Cool turquoise colors are a total contrast to marmalade (**1**), offering highs and lows of light and shade throughout the room.

Dramatic contrasts make for a lively environment.

Such contrasting combinations are bound to provoke an emotional response. Keep accessories and decoration to a minimum – the colors are already doing all the work needed.

Cool mint (**2**) and deep turquoise (**3**) are great colors for a shower curtain, and for stained glass at the window, in the cabinet door or in a light fixture.

Ruby (**4**) and blood orange (**5**) offer even hotter colors for items such as towels, plant pots and mirror frames.

Bashful, *shy and delicate*

Modest colors suited to a living room or conservatory.

These colors are reminiscent of a bygone era when ladies retired to their own room for activities such as needlepoint or poetry reading. Today such delicacies can be revived for a calm and meditative environment in the home. Use tangerine (**1**) alone or with the other colors in painted stripes.

Orange blossom (**2**) will probably be used in almost equal amounts to the main orange. This will maintain an air of sensitivity, so the orange does not overpower the rest of room.

Blond (**3**) can be used for pale wood furniture, wicker chairs and polished, pale wood flooring.

Mix these two quite similar shades of cool green (**4**, **5**) in a polka-dot fabric for seat cushions, curtains and fabric-covered lampshades.

Source antique china for afternoon tea with orange-blossom cakes and cucumber sandwiches.

Polka dot *geometric*

These tones are inspired by the modern, geometric patterns of textiles and ceramics from the 1950s, when orange juice (**1**) colors were mixed with lemon curd and outlined in black. Source original accessories for this room: hang a full-skirted dress above the fireplace or stack vinyl 45s on a side table.

Mix modern colors with original retro details.

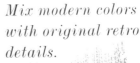

Use cotton candy (**2**) for the woodwork in the room. Strawberry sorbet (**3**) is perfect for seat covers. Mix it with the main orange in polka-dot fabric patterns.

Lemon curd (**4**) is a great contrast color in this room. Use it in details in a kitchen, such as on tea towels, breakfast bowls or even a bright toaster, juicer or coffee machine.

Black (**5**) is used as a linear motif throughout this design. All colors are mixed in retro ceramicware, Bakelite utensils, and fun, original 1950s packaging tins left on show.

Peach *champagne cocktail*

A cocktail of contemporary colors, from soft to neon.

Peach champagne (**1**) is combined with steely grays and neon fuchsia. In true eclectic style we have mixed and matched our inspirations and come up with a very modern look. Use this palette in a bedroom, bathroom or even a study with lots of glass and natural light.

1

2

3

Steel (**2**) can be used for super-soft velvet chairs and sofas. Paint the woodwork and floor with pale iced blue (**3**) and use steel-colored sheepskin rugs as an alternative to carpet in the bedroom or bathroom. In a study use the iced blue as a calming element by painting the desk and bookshelves.

4

5

Good quality cotton in rich fuchsia (**4**) can be used for bedding. Accent this with contrasting satin cushions.

Use the neon pink (**5**) for lighting, fun pen or toothbrush holders, and for drawer handles.

Gentle, *whitened and light*

A wonderfully pale combination of colors is accented with a sharp injection of true orange. This contrasting use of colors brings out the tones of the main shade, nectar (**1**). Use this palette in a bedroom or kitchen for a feminine, yet modern take on pastels.

Softened pastel colors for a soothing, mild environment.

1

2

3

Summer-sky blue (**2**) is a fresh and uplifting color to be used for soft furnishings and carpets.

Tranquil green (**3**) can be used in flat paint for woodwork, kitchen cupboards and any external doors in the room.

Dusky lavender (**4**) is less clean than the other colors in the room. It is a great shade for heavy wovens or sueded fabric to cover chairs.

4

5

Use bold signal orange (**5**) in prints on the walls or in patterned cushions and ceramic bowls.

Dusty, *faded and matte*

Drama can be found in almost colorless colors.

A very clever use of colors – it takes real confidence to opt for a palette where the colors are pale and washed out. Subtle use of color can easily be as dramatic as bold combinations. Mix textures and surfaces in this room to enhance the delicate peaches and cream (**1**) shades.

1

2

3

Dusty mauve (**2**) and sugared almond (**3**) are pretty, antiqued colors, perfect for jacquard fabrics on chairs and cushions. Choose regency-inspired, swirling patterns in combinations of light and shade.

4

Pistachio ice cream (**4**) is the perfect shade for painted floorboards, window shutters and sills, and baseboards.

5

Choose pale khaki (**5**) to mix with the other colors for fabric patterns or for a single area of wallpaper. It can be a great focus in a room to simply paper a chimney breast in a bold, floral or geometric pattern.

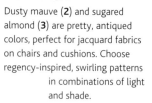

Orange cream *and sweet balm*

Sweet orange mousse (**1**) could be taken into a totally feminine palette, but here it is used in a traditional range based on natural hues and historic color combinations. Delicate lemon and soft, deep browns mix together to create a cozy country kitchen that easily translates into 21st century style.

Kitchen colors scented with orange and lemon balm.

Toffee (**2**) and butterscotch (**3**) are rich, homely colors perfectly suited to the cooking environment. Use them in the form of orange-hued woods, such as cherry or beech, for kitchen cupboards or an informal scrubbed dining table and chairs.

Lemon meringue (**4**) is a light and fluffy color perfect for lace curtains and feather-filled chair cushions.

Use deep ebony (**5**) for the stone or wood flooring for an elegant but practical finish. Complete the look with fruit and serving bowls carved from dark wood.

Natural *oranges and blues*

Striking natural pigments from earth tones to lapis lazuli.

Brick (**1**) is a natural complement to blue. Painters once had to source natural pigments and mix their own paints. Lapis lazuli came from Afghanistan and was more expensive than gold. It produced the most brilliant of blues and was made famous by the Venetian artist Titian.

This palette would work well in a bathroom, kitchen or dining room. Use traditional Moroccan tadelakt, a lime-based, water-resistant plaster, on the walls.

Use a darker terra cotta shade (**2**) for the natural baked-tile flooring. Rich, Turkish red (**3**) is perfect for kitchen cupboards and wood.

Intense blues like cobalt and lapis lazuli (**4**, **5**) are perfect for heavy, woven fabrics for curtains and seat covers. Source tiles with the traditional, rich-blue patterning from Africa or Andalusia for an authentic look.

Delicious, *luxurious and sensual*

This is an incredibly sexy palette and could work just as well in a living room as in a bedroom. Irresistible shades of caramel (**1**), hot chocolate and chestnut are enlivened with rich, succulent injections of plum and purpled suede. Use good quality materials in this room.

Rich coloration ensures a seductive environment.

Use the softest and most luxurious surfaces in here, such as matte, powdery paint finishes for the walls. Cashmere, suede and velvet are perfect indulgences to mix and match for furniture, curtains and cushions. Invest in fine touches, such as hand-blocked wallpaper on one wall or an oversized antique mirror above the fireplace.

Use the chocolate shades (**2**, **3**) for heavy furniture and period details in the room. Plum (**4**) and purple fig (**5**) are wonderful shades for fabrics and glassware.

Linear *and well designed*

Unobtrusive colors perfect for clean, modern designs.

This is a clean, simple style reminiscent of the 1950s. Walnut (**1**) is perfect for a stylized dining room. When using drab colors, the design ethics have to be strict for the palette to work. As designer and poet William Morris said, "have nothing in your houses that you do not know to be useful or believe to be beautiful."

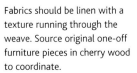

Fabrics should be linen with a texture running through the weave. Source original one-off furniture pieces in cherry wood to coordinate.

These similar shades of straw (**2**, **3**) are perfect to use in stripes for fabrics. Also, use the paler of the two colors for woodwork and door frames.

Soft khaki (**4**) is the darkest shade within the room. Use it for the carpet and large seat covers.

Putty (**5**) is a great tinted neutral. Mix it with the other colors in 1950s-style furnishing fabrics or in original paperback books.

Masculine, *chic and smart*

Source traditional suit fabrics, such as tweed, herringbone and even Scottish tartan, for an alternative material to cover seats and sofas. Use these natural wools to inspire the color scheme for the room. Saffron (**1**) is a sophisticated, natural foundation on which to build this palette.

A formal palette inspired by gentlemen's tailors.

This palette would work well in a study or living–dining area. The colors are smart and tailored, but the bold saffron orange offers a sense of fun.

Bark (**2**) and bracken (**3**) are wonderfully deep, natural colorations, perfect for furniture, deep baseboards, and around the fireplace.

Air-force blue (**4**) is a cool accent among these warm shades. Mix it in the weave for fabrics and furnishings, or use it for picture frames.

Turmeric (**5**) is a bright highlight that can be used for corduroy cushions and light fixtures.

Sweet icing *and sugared almonds*

Harmonious sugar-coated pastels subdue hot orange.

Hot candied peel (**1**) is mellowed slightly with a flat, whitened finish, so use eggshell paint and natural fabrics to soften the impact of the bold color. These aromatic colors are washed out to prevent the room from becoming sharp or sickly.

Soft pistachio (**3**) is perfect for a contrast color on woodwork. If the green is too contrasted, white will lighten the overall feel. Use white on the woodwork, and mix it in stripes or checks with the pistachio and dusty mauve (**2**) for fabrics, furnishings and carpets. This palette could work well in a bedroom or living room.

Peach and toffee (**4**, **5**) are great colors for details. Use on light fixtures, candlesticks and bowls for fruit, jewelry or flowers.

Mix *cosmopolitan with country*

A bold and modern palette that could work well in a new or old building and is perfect for a contemporary yet practical kitchen space or a rustic country bedroom. Ginger (**1**) gives a homely feel to any room, and mixing it with peony pinks breaks away from the traditional terra-cotta and yellow combination.

Warm and cool colors contrast for a rustic yet modern look.

Two shades of peony (**2**, **3**) are wonderfully rich and decorative colors that look great as blocks of flat color on kitchen cupboards or surfaces. Mix them with the cool shades below on modern florals or graphic printed fabrics.

Porcelain tint (**5**) and ice blue (**4**) bring contrast to the palette. These cool colors help to prevent this room from becoming too pretty or too traditional.

Go for a mixture of accessories from worn and loved, faded armchairs to modern glass shelving and lampshades.

Coffee *and after-dinner mint*

A dining room for entertaining should be elegant but fun.

The finest shades of coffee (**1**) and chocolate are perfect for any dining area. Exquisitely rich and instantly gratifying, brown tones create a feeling of warmth in any room. Accessorize with quirky dinner plates in bright mint and cutlery made from fake tortoiseshell or polished coconut.

Espresso (**2**) is a darker version of the main color. Use it for the woodwork and dining table. For an unusual touch, paint vertical stripes of espresso with fudge (**3**) along the length of the table.

Use bright mint (**4**) and mint (**5**) in fabrics for chair seats and curtains. For a modern fireplace, use mint tiles. Source recycled green glass tumblers and goblets.

Serve mint martinis or mint tea with fresh mint leaves, and make mint chocolate mousse in green Moroccan tea glasses.

Nutmeg, *tea and pumpkin*

When designing any environment, you must take into account all five senses. Colors can stimulate us visually, but use scents of cinnamon and nutmeg (**1**) or freshly-baked pumpkin pie for a complementing scent and taste sensation. Search for fabrics that demand to be stroked and play uplifting music.

A stimulating palette that arouses all the senses.

Rich nutmeg (**1**) is a sexy base color upon which to build a palette. These colors would transform a tired kitchen or dining area.

Aqua (**2**) and robin's-egg blue (**3**) both offer a bright and softened accent. Use them in varying degrees depending on your taste for intense colors.

Honey (**4**) can be used for curtains and picture or mirror frames. Mix honey with robin's egg and amber (**5**) in fine-striped fabrics for seat covers, cushions, and quirky tea cups and plates.

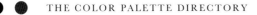

Chestnut *and saddle*

A traditional brown is enlivened with hot flame colors.

The classic color of leather (**1**) is underappreciated in interior design. This rich and expensive-looking shade is incredibly versatile. Mix it with simple, neutral shades for a timeless, conservative look, or use bright accents for a modern edge.

Café latte (**2**) and coffee cream (**3**) are perfect accent shades, blending easily with the main color. Use these warm, creamy tones on woodwork and fabrics, such as suedes and leathers, for upholstery. Mix these colors in an ice-cream swirl for contemporary, cast-resin furniture, such as tables and side chairs.

Many modern accent colors would work here, such as violet or turquoise. Flame red and flame orange (**4**, **5**) offer a spicy touch. Utilize these colors in accessories such as cushions and lampshades in Chinese silk.

Elegant, *understated neutrals*

Rich tea (**1**) is beautifully complemented by these soft tints of
powdered heritage colors, making the new neutrals very elegant.
This deeply luxurious palette is perfect for a sensuous boudoir
or a wonderfully indulgent bathroom. Use a soft,
pinked tone on the wall behind the bed to
lift the dark brown.

*Tinted natural
shades enhance this
rich, deep brown.*

Soft pink (**2**) is the main accent
color and can be used almost as
much as tea (**1**). Use it in a flat
finish on the walls and contrast
in high gloss for the woodwork
and for wood paneling in
a bathroom.

The soft browns (**3**, **4**, **5**)
are pretty yet
sophisticated. Use for
satin cushions, a tinted
glass chandelier and
mismatched bowls.

Accessorize with decorative,
antique, French-style furniture
and monogrammed bed linen
and towels. Use an old, curved,
wrought-iron garden chair
for seating.

Yellows

Seasoned, *masculine and polished*

A palette for a gentleman's study or sitting room.

These easy tan colors are inviting and relaxing. A sophisticated palette of golden ocher (**1**) and warm, natural colors is perfect for a workroom or study area. Look to surfaces used in museums and libraries, such as wood paneling, buttoned leather and even linen wall-coverings.

Rich, golden ocher is softened with muted accent colors for a luxurious feel. For a quality finish choose natural paints made from traditional earth pigments. These paints will last a long time and have a milder odor compared to their chemical counterparts.

Straw (**2**) and string (**3**) are versatile colors that offer a true classic finish.

Chestnut (**4**) is a perfect color for leather chairs and a leather-covered writing desk. Mix straw, string and sand (**5**) in textiles for a floor rug and heavy velvet curtains. Cover a single area of the wall with natural linen wallpaper.

Ripened *country corn*

Tones of ripened corn (**1**) evoke long summer days and warm evenings. Such natural colors are perfect for country houses, cottages and older character buildings. These yellows would also work well on the exterior of a house. Use them for a cozy kitchen or solarium.

Rich, egg-yolk yellows inspire a warm ambience.

Choosing yellows with a warm, orange glow gives a soft touch and invokes a comfortable ambience.

Dark forest green (**2**) is a classic color to combine with ocher tones. Think of old-fashioned racing cars with corn (**3**) leather seating when choosing the furniture. Use forest green for a traditional farmhouse oven and for cupboard doors.

Egg yolk (**4**) and ginger (**5**) are great cooking colors to have in the kitchen, and are also natural and practical for accessories.

Bold, *desert neutrals*

Tinted neutrals and acid brights are modern and graphic.

Neutral tones are incredibly versatile. Choose a good neutral base and you can keep the color on the walls for many years – simply change the accent colors to create a totally new space with little added expense. Desert (**1**) works just as well with terra-cottas or soft greens.

1

2

3

Modern interior decorating is all about clever use of color. This does not mean that we all have to go for vibrant pigments. It has become the height of contemporary interior design fashion to choose beautiful, tinted neutral tones throughout the house.

4

5

Rabbit (**2**) and warm gray (**3**) are subtle colors that work well because they have a warm glow to them.

To keep the room from becoming drab, acid lime (**4**) is used sparingly on fabric patterns and accessories. Slate (**5**) gives a dark outline for details and finishes.

A Côte d'Azur *tanned classic*

Beach sand (**1**), bronzed bodies and the azure ocean create a perfectly harmonious palette. This classic yellow tone is given a new direction with clever use of color in the accessories and woodwork. Brown and azure always look good together, be it in interior design or fashion.

Inspired by the colors of the Mediterranean.

The secondary colors of tan (**2**) and chestnut brown (**3**) give richness to the main yellow. This palette would work well in a living or dining area with 1950s-style wooden furniture in walnut or cherry.

Dusty green (**4**) and azure (**5**) are wonderful accessory colors for velvet cushions and gorgeous ceramics.

When looking for fabric for the interior be inventive. Visit tailors instead of upholsterers to source traditional tweeds and wools for covering chairs.

Sunshine *play*

Use primary colors in a fun room for family and friends.

This vibrant sunshine yellow (**1**) is fun and enlivening. Such a clean primary color can be used for a children's play area or any room used for entertaining. With accents of ice-cream colors and primary blues, this palette utilizes opposing cool and warm tones.

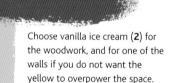

Choose vanilla ice cream (**2**) for the woodwork, and for one of the walls if you do not want the yellow to overpower the space.

Raspberry ripple (**3**) is a fantastic color for plastic chairs or fun beanbag chairs. Any upholstery and flooring in this room should be easy to clean as there will be a lot of traffic passing through.

Elementary blues such as navy (**5**) and china blue (**4**) are perfect partners to rich yellow. Use them for cushions, curtains and wooden storage crates to tidy away all the children's toys.

Spring crocus *and cowslips*

These colors would be perfect to wake up to in the morning. Lemon cake (**1**) is sweet and charming while daybreak tones of sunlight yellow and new-shoot green are fresh and uplifting. Utilize this palette in a bedroom, bathroom or kitchen for an instant morning glow.

A light and airy palette inspired by spring meadows.

1

2

3

Pretty ivory (**2**) is a perfect color for curtains and will let the morning rays of sun filter into the room naturally. Use this color for woodwork and even on painted floorboards to increase the lightness of the room.

4

Sprightly mint (**3**) is a really fresh green. Paint it over wooden furniture such as chairs and cupboards. Alternatively, choose it for breakfast plates in the kitchen.

5

Fern green (**4**) and peach (**5**) can be used for delicate, floral prints or embroidery on bed linen, towels or upholstery fabrics.

Honey *and vanilla cream*

Sweet and sensuous pastry colors are richly indulgent.

A delectable color palette of honey (**1**), rich vanilla cream and hot chocolate is brought up to date when accessorized with intense and sensuous raspberry and neon pink. This palette would work well in a living room or bedroom; it is classic yet fun.

The main colors in this room of honey (**1**) and cream (**2**) are simply elegant.

Chocolate brown (**3**) is no longer a color for traditionalists. Use this rich tone for the floors and for modern, low tables. Fabrics can be chocolate with graphic prints in bright pink mixed with cream. In the bedroom why not try a chocolate, fake fur throw on the bed?

Choose raspberry (**4**) and neon pink (**5**) for eye-catching accessories, such as a single designer chair or dark pink roses in cream ceramic vases.

Diverse, *neat and tidy*

This unconventional color combination works well because of the washed-out, or dusty, quality of the main colors. The main faded buttercup (**1**) is the type of color that could really work throughout the home. It is neutral enough to make a perfect background, yet energetic enough to create atmosphere.

A strong mix of colors needs a lack of clutter.

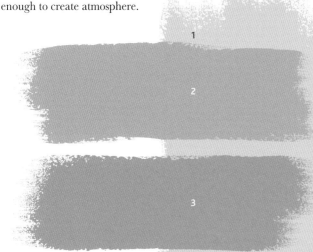

Pale lilac (**2**) and cool amethyst (**3**) are tints of color that perfectly balance with the main buttercup tone. Use these shades for floors and large pieces of furniture.

Muted yellow (**4**) and mandarin (**5**) offer brighter highlights within the room while still complementing the main shade.

Mix all the highlight colors together in quirky, Chanel-inspired, textured, woven fabrics for chairs and sofas.

A sunny *rose garden*

This modern vintage feel is all about the feminine details.

A bright, sunny bathroom in pretty yellow rose (**1**) is perfectly accessorized in colors from the rose garden. Choose reclaimed furniture for this room: a traditional free-standing bath tub, original faucet fittings and stripped wooden chairs and cabinets. Surfaces have a flat, faded finish.

1

2

3

Light khaki (**2**) and pistachio (**3**) are perfect colors for a flat wood-work finish. Wooden paneling in the bathroom can be painted the same color as the cupboards, window frames and towel bars.

4

5

Cover an old chair with striped fabric in rose (**4**) and geranium (**5**), and use the same fabric for curtains and tiebacks.

Accessorize with a reproduction ceramic floral soap dish and water jug for a vintage feel. You could also source pink glycerin soaps and bath products with floral fragrances.

Salon *star treatment*

Choose surfaces carefully, and contrast glossy and smooth textures to exaggerate soft lemon (**1**) tints. With well-chosen French-style furniture and accessories, you could create a real salon feel. Lots of light is needed in this room at all times of day in order to differentiate between the colors.

A delightful medley of pastels creates a soft, pretty mood.

1

2

3

Flat, lemon yellow walls are challenged when set against the lacquered finish of mint (**2**) and soft sage green (**3**) for glossy woodwork and shelving.

Use pale pink (**4**) and soft peach (**5**) velvet for quilting. Sheepskin and sequinned cushions add depth, luxury and texture. Hang a sparkly chandelier in this room for a truly decadent salon experience.

4

5

For a totally glamorous approach, look for a pink- or peach-tinted mirror to use as a tabletop or, alternatively, frame it with dressing-room light bulbs for that superstar treatment.

Subtle, *cool and relaxing*

Stylish, refined colors for a dining room or work area.

Natural wheat (**1**) is great for plain walls, or for painting over textured wallpaper, such as woven fabric or fine, vertical, textured stripes. This palette of soft yellow, white, and cool blue gray is a modern, paler interpretation of a traditional interior look. It invokes a calming and hospitable atmosphere.

1

2

3

You may say that white (**2**) is not a color, but here we are using white woodwork as a partner to soft yellow to keep the look clean and graphic.

Pale, dusty blue (**3**) is a fantastic color for upholstery. Choose a textured fabric such as velvet, heavy wovens or even knitted surfaces for an unusual touch.

4

5

Modern accessories in slate blue (**4**) and gun-metal gray (**5**) should have simple shapes with minimal decoration. Choose square, Japanese-style dining plates and narrow, extra-tall vases to stand out against the pale yellow walls.

Cosmetic *cream and powder*

Cream (**1**) is often a prettier alternative to pure white, and here it is mixed in a delicious blend with skin tones of peach sorbet, butterscotch and rose pink. Deliciously feminine and aromatic, these tones could be used in almost any combination. It is a perfect palette for the bedroom that works just as well in the kitchen.

A palette inspired by fragrant makeup.

Just like applying makeup, build the layers of this room gradually until the perfect finish is achieved.

Pressed powder (**2**) and sweet biscuit (**3**) are great foundation colors. Use these feminine neutrals for the flooring and bed covers; in the kitchen paint the cabinets in a flat or eggshell finish.

Blush pink (**4**) can be used for selected fabric embellishment.

Rich butterscotch (**5**) is a strong color and must be used sparingly, perhaps only on cupboard handles and glassware.

Hints of lemon; *lush, graphic*

Fresh lemon and rich mid-tones in a luxurious blend.

Citrus (**1**) is a lime-based tinted yellow and the perfect ground for a lush palette of fern greens and orchid mauves. Use the main color and the two green accent tones to complement each other, like shadows, in alcoves and on the chimney breast. This pretty palette could work in any room.

1

2

3

Limeade (**2**) and fern (**3**) are perfect yellow-based greens. By cleverly combining these two different depths of color with the main color, a contemporary and graphic look can be achieved. Always use masking tape when painting different colors next to each other in order to maintain sharp lines.

4

5

Use the pretty tones of orchid (**4**) and sweet pea (**5**) in striped fabrics for curtains and cushions. Source tropical orchids in similar colors, and place three identical plants in the center of a low table for a sleek finish.

Sherbet: *zingy and sparkling*

This super-pale, lemon sherbet (**1**) is light and airy, giving a zesty lift to any tired bedroom or bathroom. Use it to breathe new life into dark areas and rooms that do not get a lot of daylight. Yellow and blue is a classic yet exhilarating combination. Consider glitter paints for details.

A classic color combination with a light twist.

1

2

3

These blues have been carefully selected for a clean, fresh feeling. Bright aqua (**3**) and Wedgwood blue (**2**) are at quite different ends of the blue scale, yet sit happily together with the sherbet. Use the blues for woodwork and to match tiling in a bathroom.

4

The accent colors in this palette are soft and in contrast with the brighter main colors. By accessorizing in grayed shades of blue, the overall look of the room does not become too naive or kitsch. Use duck egg (**4**) and soft clay (**5**) for fabrics and fixtures.

5

Hot *Indian summer*

Fiery colors create a hot Bollywood experience.

Yellow gold (**1**) is combined with a range of super-hot oranges for a glowing palette inspired by Bollywood. Vibrant, expressive and fun, this palette can either be used as inspiration or taken to a fully themed environment with sari curtains and glitzy details.

Use sunset orange (**3**) and peach puff (**2**) for tinted Formica surfaces on tabletops.

For a really kitsch touch, have a collection of Bollywood movie posters printed onto Formica and use them for tabletop surfaces or wall hangings.

Transparent, traditional Indian sari fabrics in hot marigold (**4**) are perfect as an alternative to curtains and for cushion covers. Source garlands of paper flowers to drape from the curtain rods and over the mantelpiece.

Fill deep glass bowls in rich eggplant (**5**) with brightly colored traditional Indian candies and toys.

Whimsical, *mystical shimmer*

Shimmering lily (**1**) is almost dreamlike in its ethereal quality. Such a pale and fragile color will lift any room, giving it a light and dreamy atmosphere. Mix with a palette of dragonfly greens and deep-forest violets for a fantasy bathroom perfect for long, secret baths.

Surreal contrasts of lemon and green for a fairy-tale bathroom.

Surreal, dragonfly-wing greens (**2**, **3**) are the perfect colors for translucent surfaces such as glass and tinted plastics, or for an opaque or frosted shower curtain or free-standing room screen. For a really adventurous look, paint a pattern of fantasy climbing plants onto the screen or wall in darker peacock (**4**).

You can mix all four accent colors together for patterned fabrics. Use violet (**5**) for details, such as feathers instead of flowers in a vase. Invest in pieces of amethyst or malachite for unusual ornamentation.

Clear, *fresh and energetic*

Revitalizing colors that almost take your breath away.

Mix brilliant crayon yellow (**1**) with active blues and spearmint for a dynamic palette, great for any lively room. You can make use of artificial colors just as often as naturally influenced tones, and such vivid, modern paints should be celebrated for their totally contemporary appeal.

1

2

3

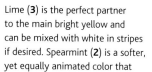

4

5

Lime (**3**) is the perfect partner to the main bright yellow and can be mixed with white in stripes if desired. Spearmint (**2**) is a softer, yet equally animated color that can be used for floors and woodwork.

Clean turquoise (**4**) is great for a fun children's bedroom or play area. Use it for plastic seating, or for the bedframe.

Cornflower blue (**5**) is traditionally a favorite color for a boy's room. Mixed with these other fresh colors, cornflower becomes a graphic accent color useful for picture frames. Try painting racing stripes around the room.

Light and lavish *lime*

This luminous palette of lime yellow (**1**) and rich, botanical jungle greens would make an intense and decadent living space. If possible choose a room that opens directly onto the yard. Greened tones are layered from soft pea through to deep olive.

Succulent mouth-watering limes and overgrown greens.

Deepest olive (**2**) is a luscious color to use in combination with lime yellow (**1**) on glossy woodwork in a living room. Paint wooden blinds or shutters at the windows for a colonial style.

Paradise pink (**3**) is a much needed respite from all the green in the room. Use it in fabric patterns and for fruit bowls and dinner and side plates.

Electric limes (**4**, **5**) should be used sparingly in fabrics and on lampshades.

Mix the colors together in retro-style, giant, floral-patterned fabrics for a kitsch touch on cushions and covered footstools.

Art deco: *classic good taste*

Use historical color references for a touch of instant style.

Putty (**1**) is typical of some of the first interior paint colors produced in the early 20th century. A classic color, it works equally well in a period property or a modern, open-plan space. Accessorize with geometric chrome on kitchen appliances and table and chair legs.

This palette is inspired by the art deco period which was a fantastic time for design and innovation. Putty (**1**) is underlined with a strong use of black (**2**). Black woodwork looks great on traditional windows and simply gorgeous on extra-deep baseboards. Alternatively, opt for black glass surfaces.

Warm 1920s pink (**3**) adds a touch of glamor to the palette.

Nile green (**4**) was the epitome of fashion during this period. Use with nut brown (**5**) in furnishings and details to complete this look. Source original art deco furniture and authentic textile prints.

Bamboo *and chinoiserie style*

Bamboo (**1**) is used all over the world for making furniture, flooring and lightweight utensils; it also grows quickly and is environmentally friendly. The subtle tones of bamboo make the perfect inspiration for a warm, background color. Be inspired by the influence of Chinese art on early 19th-century interiors.

Earthy pigments and finishings create an Eastern look.

Intense lacquered red (**2**) can be varnished or glazed after painting to recreate the traditional Chinese finish to woodwork. Use for doors and oversized wooden cupboards or armoires. Source heavy, unpolished brass knobs and handles for an authentic feel, and accessorize with red or yellow silk tassels.

Brick red (**3**) is the perfect color for fabrics. Choose either decorative Chinese jacquards or plain velvet.

Rich earth (**4**) and lucky yellow (**5**) can be used in Chinese-style patterns and ornaments.

Girly, *mischievous, flirtatious*

Flirt with color in a merry mix of tongue-in-cheek brights.

Decorating your home should be enjoyable so really let your personality shine through in the colors you choose. Natural, fruity colors like pear (**1**) always make people smile. Let rooms in your home become an extension of your wardrobe by filling them with favorite colors.

1

2

3

Flamboyant floral colors mix easily in a happy room. Choose lemon-lime meringue (**2**) for the woodwork, doors and ceiling coving to soften the edges of this lively environment.

Leaf green (**3**) could be used to paint furniture, such as kitchen chairs or cupboard doors.

4

5

Use bubble gum (**5**) and jawbreaker (**4**) as candy colors for seat covers. Find funky kitchen accessories, like rubber gloves, tea towels and a broom and dustpan to hang on the wall, in these bright shades.

Chamomile *infusion*

Chamomile (**1**) gets a classic finish when combined with tea browns. This palette works in a living room, dining area or open-plan kitchen. Warmed colors melt together to create an instantly cozy atmosphere perfect for sunny mornings or winter evenings around the fire.

Cuddle up in warm, comforting tones of yellow and tea.

Tea (**2**) is the major secondary color. Use it for the flooring and a large, family dining table.

Wholemeal (**3**) is a rather sophisticated color but it adds a needed element of neutrality to curtains and work surfaces.

Accessorize with battered, old leather armchairs and hand-knitted blankets or patchwork throws. Stack chopped firewood in an unused grate or along the wall as a feature.

Use tobacco (**4**) and begonia (**5**) in fabrics and hand-painted ceramics.

Illustrative, *off-beat and visual*

A computer-generated palette for modern interiors.

A contrasting palette of lights and darks that is inspired by modern graphic illustration. Look for nightclub flyers or business cards from trendy shops and imitate their contemporary use of muted color with flashes of highlight. Willow (**1**) is a safe color on which to build this unpredictable scheme.

Natural colors are improved upon here with man-made techniques. Dusky rose (**2**) and jungle (**3**) are richer, sharper versions of their natural origins. Use jungle for the woodwork and dusky rose for flooring and designer furniture.

Garnet (**4**) is the all-important underlining color in this room. Use in graphic patterns on wallpaper, cushions, serving plates and wall posters.

Use sunset orange (**5**) for modern lighting and an entertainment center that hangs on the wall like a painting.

Sun-ripened *Nordic blond*

This classic range of colors is inspired by Scandinavian land-scapes. Northern light makes colors look cool and clear, and these countries are historically more likely to opt for cool interior shades. Great for a kitchen or bathroom, blond (**1**) and blue are basic shades with a twist.

Everyday colors for a lively yet restorative palette.

Blond (**1**) can be used in fabric wall-coverings or painted over textured paper.

Corn (**2**) is a cleaner, more primary yellow to be used for the window frames and will exaggerate any sunlight that filters through. Use pea green (**3**) for kitchen cupboards and bathroom cabinets.

Teal (**4**) and petrol blue (**5**) are perfect for furnishing fabrics. Choose corduroy for seat covers and pick curtains with unusual textures.

Source Nordic landscape paintings to tie the color scheme together.

Greens

Natural, *balanced forest*

Mix light and dark greens to restore a room's equilibrium.

Green is the color in the center of the rainbow and the color wheel, and for this reason it is said to be a balancing color. The color of nature, the forest (**1**) and new growth, green is also a restorative color that can lift the spirit. Use green in a dining area to create a comfortable yet invigorating environment.

If dark green is the predominant color in a room, you will need to have pale shades to prevent the room from becoming too overbearing. Celery (**2**) is a perfect color to balance dark green. In a traditional house use the darker color below the chair rail and palest celery above.

Soft fern (**3**) is a great color for the floor – either choose a good quality carpet or paint the floorboards.

Dark forest (**4**) can be used for the baseboards and window frames to create an outline. Pale mint (**5**) is a fun highlight for cushions.

Bloomsbury *style*

Charleston House in Suffolk, England, is a historical landmark and a celebration of the talents of the artists and writers (Virginia Woolf was one) who lived there in the early 20th century. The house was painted in colors like emerald (**1**), now synonymous with the 1920s.

Colors inspired by the famous Bloomsbury set.

The main dark, yellowed green is brought to life when combined with these dusty, mid-tone colors. Let your imagination run wild with these hues and paint patterns on the doors, tabletops and even the floor.

Celadon green (**2**) is a great soft, neutral color upon which to build the remaining colors. Use it for the floor.

Dusty rose (**3**) and Tuscan orange (**4**) can be used for patterned fabrics.

Olive (**5**) is a wonderfully rich green that is perfect for painting furniture.

Spring-fresh *floral*

Leafy green is a perfect background to petal shades.

Leaf (**1**) is a yellow-based, natural shade of green that takes reference from the garden. We should never overlook Mother Nature's use of color as our primary source of inspiration. This palette can have a seasonal twist with more pale pink in summer and rich purple in winter.

1

2

3

Use the main leaf (**1**) green for the walls. In a small room this dark shade may seem a little oppressive, so mix with lily (**2**) on a single wall or on half walls split by a chair rail.

With such dark walls, you will need to use a paler shade for the floor and ceiling. The more adventurous designer could paint the floor in petal pink (**3**).

4

5

Lavender and purple (**4**, **5**) are perfect for upholstery and curtains to bring some real color into the room. If you want only a touch of purple then use this for the cushions and choose leaf-green furniture.

Pea and lime, *energetic and juicy*

This is not a palette for the fainthearted. A zingy mix of refreshing greens is vigorous and powerful, bringing new life and lots of energy into an area. Pea (**1**), the main green, is fresh and strong and would work well in an area with lots of traffic, such as a hall or stairwell.

Revive a tired space in the home with invigorating brights.

Pampas grass (**2**) is a light, yellowed green that could be used for painting a wooden floor or for staining pale woods such as pine.

Sage (**3**) is a great color for fabrics and upholstery. Choose heavy wovens to make a curtain across the front door to keep out the cold.

Lime (**4**) is a striking accent color that is great for fun details. Choose transparent materials, such as glass or resins.

Forest (**5**) can be used for a rug and for picture frames to give a darker level and ground this vivid palette.

Muted, *quiet and tranquil*

A meditative mix of softened greens and cool, subdued blues.

Green has been said to have meditative qualities. These softened, grayed-off tones are perfect for a simple, composed atmosphere in any area of the home. Avocado (**1**) evokes an instant feeling of well-being for a bathroom, and it will induce a peaceful sleep in the bedroom.

Choose natural materials in this room. If possible source natural pigment-based paints, such as limewash or distemper. These paints are not only good for your home and the environment, they also have an unmistakable natural, flat quality.

Use cool blue and gray blue (**2**, **3**) in a flat finish to wash wooden cupboards and paneling. If you have a wooden floor use these shades to stain it.

Spearmint (**5**) brings a fresh injection of color perfect for fabrics, curtains, towels and bedcovers in crisp cotton.

Modern *graphic contrasts*

This is a playful collaboration of brights and darks. Opposing colors are placed next to each other for dramatic contrast. Green and red are opposites on the color wheel, but can have a striking effect when used together, as seen here with lime (**1**), peacock (**4**) and burned orange (**5**).

A contemporary mix of strong colors for a fun interior.

These colors are perfect to bring some life into an open-plan, industrial-style living space. Such bold color combinations will draw the eye in. This is also a great palette for a children's play area with strong sports connotations. You could really play with stripes and color blocking on the walls and floor.

Lime (**1**) is the main color, but the bigger the area, the more the other colors can be utilized.

Use burned orange (**5**) like a warning color to signal the corners of the room or create arrows that lead the eye.

Chintz: *flowery and traditional*

A summer palette of floral colors for a feminine interior.

Red and green can work well together. Being opposite each other on the color wheel, red really stands out from the main mint ice cream (**1**) color so you may only need a small amount to make an impression. White is very important in this mix since it stops the colors from clashing.

The main green is rather strong, so antique ivory (**2**) and pink (**3**) can be used to balance the intensity. For a vintage approach use white-and-green striped wallpaper.

This room should focus around floral patterns that will mix all five colors. Source some fantastic, ultra-modern fabrics and wall-coverings in rose and flower patterns.

Lipstick red (**4**) is to be used sparingly – a single red glass for example.

Moss green (**5**) can be used for larger furniture to balance the prettiness of the room.

Romantic *ballet*

Degas painted ballet dancers rehearsing and while backstage. He used layers of delicate greens and pinks to create a light, diffused effect. Inspiration can be taken from these fragile layers of color. Gooseberry (**1**) is perfect for a graceful bedroom or a light and airy living room or solarium.

Soft colors inspired by the painter Degas.

1

2

3

The main gooseberry (**1**) is the strongest of all the colors here. Layer the four remaining colors slowly within the room, as if you are an artist creating a masterpiece.

Use palest fennel (**2**) for the ceiling and floor. Dusty plaster (**3**) is a perfect, neutral shade to use for large pieces of furniture, such as the sofa and armchairs.

4

5

Mix layers of organza in powder peach (**4**) and ballet pink (**5**) for an unusual window dressing. Also, use the pink for satin-covered cushions and hang a Degas print above the fireplace.

Open *garden*

Bring the outside in with garden-inspired, fresh, light colors.

Make the living space feel like it is a part of the garden by choosing leafy greens and pistachio (**1**), light and airy neutral shades and splashes of fuchsia. Rooms that open out onto a garden can be exaggerated by opening out the wall and replacing it with sliding glass doors.

With as much natural daylight as possible coming into the house, the main fresh green will come to life and transform tired walls. Use mid-green (**2**) for the furnishings: it is a good basic, versatile color that can be changed with your moods from one season to another.

Pale-green tint (**3**) and concrete (**4**) can be used in an architectural way on beams and pillars. You could even continue the paving slabs from outside to inside.

Fuchsia (**5**) is a red-hot color, great for any accessory, such as cushions, mirror frames or flowers.

Aromatic *pine and lavender*

A fresh color like pine (**1**) not only delights the eye, but stirs the senses by invoking the wonderful scents of nature. Use tactile and textural surfaces, such as glossy plastics and fluffy mohair, to really bring the colors to life. Place sprigs of lavender on tabletops or in vases and fill the room with green, leafy plants.

A sensual palette of fresh colors that mimics nature.

1

2

3

This is a great bathroom palette with fresh tones of green, calming pales and invigorating lavender.

Choose rose tint (**2**) for the bathroom fixtures since this color can be taken in almost any direction when you need to change the room.

4

Soft lavender (**3**) is a great color for the woodwork, including the bath surround and bathroom cabinet.

5

Lavender (**4**) and pine (**5**) are strong colors so have fun with them. Visit second-hand stores for unusual china. Cover old books with wallpaper and leave them as gifts for your guests to unwrap.

Apples, *blossoms and sunlight*

Pale apple green brings us the color of spring.

Using light apple (**1**) is a great way of bringing the outside in. Greens can really lift a room, and whether you're decorating a traditional cottage or a modern apartment, pale greens suit every style. Calming and easy on the eye, sweet apple tones offer a pretty alternative for any bedroom.

1

2

3

A look inspired by new spring buds and warm summer mornings. Complete it with natural, pale-wood furniture – and always have fresh flowers on show to complement the colors.

4

Imagine the sunlight filtering through the window and capture that perfect sunny yellow (**2**) to combine with spring green (**3**) for a warming and inviting mix.

5

For a truly garden-inspired touch, use delicate highlights of apple-blossom pink (**5**) or cherry blossom (**4**) for scatter cushions and rugs.

Sorbet, *lemon meringue and fig*

This wonderful, contemporary mix of light and bright shades is inspired by desserts. Lime sorbet (**1**) is a wonderfully refreshing color. It will deepen as you apply the paint to the walls and change dramatically from day to night. All colors are given a yellowed hue in the evening with artificial light.

A mouth-watering palette of fruity colors.

1

2

3

Fig (**3**) is a great fabric color. Use it on upholstery and either go for a more glamorous feel with shiny velvet or a rustic approach with a matte, woven fabric.

Strawberry mousse (**2**) can be used for the woodwork and to exaggerate original features, such as a ceiling rose or shutters.

4

5

Sour lime and green lemon (**4**, **5**) add a sharp injection of flavor in glassware; mix within prints for fabrics and bold ceramics. Serve delicate cakes and fluffy meringue pies on brightly colored serving dishes to really get the juices flowing.

Classic, *refined Georgian*

Refer to historical interiors for good taste and design.

Greens like sea foam (**1**) have been popular interior colors for centuries, however, some of the first green pigments were poisonous. Visit stately homes or restored historic houses for inspiration – most paint companies now produce a historic range.

The greens in this palette are more blue-based than yellow. The green qualities of cedar (**2**) and copper green (**3**) are reflected in the pale sea foam (**1**) walls. Use these tones for upholstery.

Duck-egg (**4**) is a versatile shade that can be used for furniture, picture frames and even for an area of wallpaper, with sophisticated copper (**5**) patterning.

Complete the look with copper as a detail on the edge of frames, on door handles, and on candleholders and cushions.

Refreshing, *verdant, dewy*

Pale aqua (**1**) is clear and uplifting. Subtle colors can have an intense effect on a room and this green will reflect maximum light. Mix with contrasting shades of dark, bright and light colors for a graphic edge in a strictly modern yet soothing and meditative environment.

An invigorating choice of colors to lift the spirits.

1

2

3

4

5

Use bright white (**2**) to further lift the light levels of this room. If you have a small bathroom with little natural light, this color scheme is perfect. Use strong recessed spot lighting and place tiny bulbs around the mirror for a glamorous touch.

Deep, inky blue (**3**) is a wonderfully rich, luscious color. Use this on the window and door frames. Use for ceramic bowls, soaps and miscellaneous objects.

Spearmint (**4**) and bright aqua (**5**) can be used in tinted glass shelving and colored glass jars. Source bright, fluffy aqua towels for a touch of fun.

Peppermint, *chocolate and coffee*

A sugar-rush of color for a lively, but not too sweet, interior.

Peppermint (**1**) with chocolate brown is an age-old interior combination. This palette is rich and comfortable but with a tantalizing twist. The greens stimulate while the browns soothe and relax the soul. Use these colors in a living room or dining area for a stunning finish.

1

2

3

The main peppermint (**1**) is a wonderful ice cream shade that could easily be used on the outside as well as the inside of a house.

Chocolate (**2**) is a great color for luxurious feather-filled leather seating. Choose the softest leather or suede for total comfort.

4

Praline (**3**) is a wonderful creamy, nutty brown that would be great for woodwork and to paint an ornate fireplace.

5

Roast coffee (**5**) is for the dark-wood furniture – keep shapes modern and simple.

Use mint leaf (**4**) for details, such as cushions, rugs and glassware.

Urban *cityscape*

It is not only the natural landscape that can inspire an artist or designer. Modern cityscapes are bursting with color and design inspiration too. Cool gray and architectural green (**1**) together with traffic-signal brights make for a fantastic interior color scheme for a contemporary space.

Take a moment to look at the world and be inspired.

Bring external features into the home such as polished concrete (**3**) pillars or flooring, or use sign graphics as quirky wall decorations.

Signal green (**2**) is a great color to use on a single wall or even an area of flooring in an open-plan space.

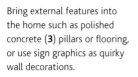

Signal red (**4**) can be utilized in many ways. Try painting stripes across the floor. Make a feature of a single piece of furniture such as a designer chair or a modern, colored, resin-coated set of drawers or sleek china cabinet.

Khaki (**5**), a great basic, can be used for the remaining furniture.

Mint, *citrus and ocean greens*

Use spearmint freshness to wake the senses.

Refreshing mint (**1**) creates a sublime yet invigorating wake-me-up bathroom palette. Light and rejuvenating blue greens have been proven to lift the spirit and clear the mind, giving a perfect start to the day.

1

2

3

Ideal for a modern bathroom or shower room, these shades need to be kept pure and distinct in order to make a real impact.

Use these lively colors with chrome fittings and crisp white furniture for a fresh and contemporary feel.

4

Citrus lime greens (**2**, **3**) are used as the main accent colors for the woodwork.

5

Choose rich, deep-ocean greens (**4**, **5**) for glassware and graphic images for the walls.

Uplifting *and natural*

This fabulous pale jade (**1**) is contrasted with natural straw colors and a bright sunshine yellow. By complementing the bright tones with natural yellowed neutrals, an easy palette that would work well in a kitchen or family room is formed. Lots of daylight from large windows will help enhance the colors.

Mix bright and natural shades for energetic rooms.

1

2

3

Use jade (**1**) for the kitchen cabinets for the look of a fun 1950s-style diner.

Sunshine yellow (**2**) is often used in kitchens, but always opt for a more "orangey" yellow for instant warmth. Use this color on one or all of the walls, depending on how much you like a wake-up call in the morning.

4

5

Avocado (**3**) and string (**4**) are perfect for natural surfaces in the room, such as sisal or coir matting for the floor and basketry for storage.

Seal brown (**5**) is a warm tone that could work for upholstery, door handles and picture frames.

Saturated, *surreal and bold*

Strong colors make a bold, hyper-real statement.

Sea green (**1**) is a strong, bright green. This tone could either be mixed with softer shades for a pretty, ice-cream-sundae palette or with rich colors for an adventurous color scheme, which will have dramatic effects in any space. Make sure you keep these daring colors in balance.

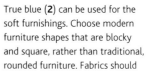

True blue (**2**) can be used for the soft furnishings. Choose modern furniture shapes that are blocky and square, rather than traditional, rounded furniture. Fabrics should be plain and simple — let the colors do all the work.

Powder blue (**3**) can be used on the woodwork.

Mauve and deep purple (**4, 5**) can be used for accessories and quirky details. Paint some unusual ornaments, such as a cast bust or a garden gnome, for weird but wonderful accessories.

Exotic *antique green*

These flat, mid-tone colors look like they have existed for many years. Soft and almost faded, verdigris (**1**), pink and neutrals conjure up many historical references. Wash the walls and use a flat finish to give the colors an aged look. Source antique, hand-printed fabrics to cover the bed or sofa.

Vintage colors from Africa and the Far East.

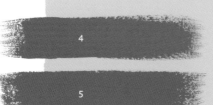

Softened pink and cashmere (**2**, **3**) are great colors for patterned fabrics, such as embroidered or hand-printed fabrics, to cover the bed or sofa.

Forest floor (**4**) can be used for natural woven floor matting or dark stained floorboards. Paint simple wooden furniture in the same color.

Use recycled green glass (**5**) for accessories, such as heavy tumblers for drinks and tea lights. Hang green glass beads in the door or at the window for a real bazaar feeling.

Enamel, *green glass and glaze*

Rich, modern greens range from softened lichen to peacock.

Green has more variations than any other color, so the possibilities and combinations for a green room are endless. With such versatility the end result can be rustic simplicity or jeweled opulence. Mix sage (**1**) in matte and shiny surfaces with enameled tiles and flat woodwork.

1

2

3

This is a great palette for a stylish and contemporary kitchen. Mix the new with the old by sourcing rustic green enamel earthenware pots and making a rich-green range oven the focus of the room.

4

Sage (**1**) and muted lichen (**2**) are the softest colors in the room and should be utilized the most.

5

In a kitchen use bright malachite (**3**) for tile or glass work surfaces and also for the tabletop.

Green tea (**4**) and peacock (**5**) are perfect for kitchen utensils, pots and glassware.

Ocean *green*

This ocean (**1**) color is very versatile. Such a shade of green could be used in a bathroom, living area or kitchen with enormous success. There are a million different ocean colors and all change with the light levels. These wonderful blue-green tones are restorative and restful.

An exciting palette of sea greens with warm reds.

Use sea foam (**3**) for the flooring. In a bathroom go for painted wooden floorboards or paint squares of plywood in different levels of green to make a checkerboard pattern.

Use shell pink (**2**) for fluffy towels and rose-colored soaps. In a living area, stripe this color with sea foam for chair covers.

Buoy red (**5**) is the accent color in the room. Use for stunning glassware or a splendid, feature chandelier.

Deep ocean (**4**) can be used for the outline, the window frame, baseboards and chair rails.

Invigorating *turquoise*

Classic colors get a twist when combined with turquoise.

Bright colors do not always have to be matched with other brights. Here, softened gray greens and midnight blues take the sharp edge off the main turquoise (**1**). This palette would make a striking statement in a dining or living room.

For a really clever approach to design, mix the unexpected together. Lightest pink (**2**) is a perfect color for upholstery. It's warm and cozy but still maintains an air of neutrality. Choose soft fabrics such as chenille, wool-mohair blends and imitation suede.

Gray green (**3**) can be used for the carpet. It could also be used on one or several of the walls if the turquoise is too much.

Bottle green and deep midnight blue (**4, 5**) give the room some depth. Use these colors for mirror frames, table settings, candlesticks and lampshades.

Sun-parched *summer meadow*

This is a rather old-fashioned group of colors. Malachite (**1**) is reminiscent of gentlemen's smoking rooms or card tables. We have mixed this stronger green with a group of softened, nostalgic shades – the kind of colors you see after a long, dry period has scorched the grasses and dried up the earth.

A subtle collection of sentimental colors faded by the sun.

Pea pod (**2**) is a pretty green that would work well for curtains and fabrics.

Sun-bleached green (**3**) can be used for woodwork, doors, window shutters and shelving.

In a kitchen, faded terra-cotta (**5**) floor tiles and work surfaces would look fantastic. Fill old terra-cotta plant pots with meadow flowers, such as daisies, poppies and sweet peas.

Shell (**4**) can be used for the kitchen cabinets and for upholstery. Mix with the other accent colors in pretty floral patterns or soft, tartan checks.

Blues

Indigo: *ancient mineral*

Deep, darkest indigo is one of the oldest dyes in the world.

With its roots in the Far East, the color indigo (**1**) has always had exotic connotations. An ultramarine blue was used by the architect Louis Majorelle to decorate his home in Marrakech. That blue is now an intrinsic part of modern architecture in Morocco.

Use deepest midnight blue (**4**) for upholstery and leather surfaces in the room. Try to use as many natural materials as possible and keep the paint flat. Mix with deep, natural pigment colors such as lapis lazuli (**3**) and red earth (**2**).

Rich gold (**5**) is the perfect color to combine with solid and dark blues. Use it in a gloss or metallic finish on picture frames, mirror edges and even on baseboards or ornate crown molding for a truly decadent atmosphere. Source place mats and candlesticks in gold leaf for the dining table.

Intense, *elegant and refined*

An intense Prussian blue (**1**) still looks fresh when combined with these soft tones. Rich, dark turquoise is contrasted with palest blue grays and a shocking, raspberry highlight. For a kitchen, choose antique French-style cupboards and paint them in washes of the pale colors.

A striking play with dark and light needs a precise design.

Source pale blue-gray (**3**) stone for the floor, or use concrete as a contemporary flooring. Leave it unpolished for a more rustic look.

Cornflower (**2**) can be used for ceramics and storage jars stacked on the shelves.

Use rich raspberry (**5**) for soft furnishings and fabrics within the room. Choose either plain, woven fabrics for seat covers or stripes of the raspberry and gray (**4**).

Progressive, *modern and fresh*

A palette of clashing colors can succeed if the balance is right.

Be daring in your color choice and create a new dimension in the home. Bright turquoise (**1**) could be a cold color to use in interior design. Mix cool shades with warmer accents to create a pleasing mood. Fresh, citrus shades complement and contrast with the turquoise.

1

2

3

This color scheme is perfect for a modern, loft-style apartment, but could be just as interesting if used in a traditional interior.

Palest aqua tint (**2**) can be used for the woodwork since the main turquoise shade needs some pale tones to balance it out.

Light citrus (**3**) and wasabi (**4**) are to be mixed for the upholstery. Use either fine stripes of the two colors or, for the dining table, choose alternating colors for the chairs.

4

5

Peach (**5**) helps to warm up the palette. Use in geometric prints for cushions and curtains.

Coney Island *summer*

This wonderful, deep-sky blue (**1**) is a happy and friendly color to use in the home, and great for a bathroom, kitchen or even a fun family living room. This palette can be made as kitsch as you like. Source fairground souvenirs to display and vintage carnival snaps and fun postcards to frame on the wall.

Colors inspired by summer days at Coney Island.

2

3

Search out quirky accessories and nostalgic memorabilia and use boating rope for curtain tiebacks, light pull cords and towel bars.

It is all about the mix. Stripes of the main blue, white (**2**) and sand (**3**) can be painted on the wall or onto wood paneling for a carnival experience.

4

Salty Atlantic blue (**5**) can be used for the flooring.

5

Use bright red (**4**) for plastic or enamel cups and plates. Make them a feature by hanging them from hooks along the wall.

Soft, *safe hideaway*

These dusty shades are restful and contemplative.

This palette is subdued and softened. Slate (**1**) is a dusky color and easy on the eye. Such a palette is great for an office or quiet living area. Cocoon yourself in matte finishes that soak up exterior noises and create a peaceful haven away from the hustle and bustle of the world.

Use a thick, soft carpet in deep slate (**2**) for total comfort underfoot. Cover seating in brushed mohair, suede or cotton velour in seal gray (**3**) for a blurred finish to this cool, neutral shade.

Dusty pink (**4**) and foxglove (**5**) can be used to add feminine details and prevent it from becoming a vision of gray. These warm shades, while not overly pretty, help to create a touch of comfort within the room. Use the pinks sparingly on cushions and placed items around the room, such as a single vase or covered books.

Classic, *tailor-made comfort*

Mix soft woad blue (**1**) with warm and cozy terra-cottas and deep plum for a bold yet comfortable living room or kitchen. Blues look great with rich brown and earth tones. This combination could easily be used for a country-style or traditional Mediterranean kitchen, or a modern, bold living room.

Bring blues into a warm and inviting environment.

Use heavy, oversized furniture to match the heavy colors. Use plum (**5**) for leather chairs and luxury seat covers.

Pottery (**2**) and blue clay (**4**) are warm and inviting colors that should fit any room like a glove.

Terra-cotta (**3**) flooring has become very chic when used in modern kitchens and living areas. Source hand-made tiles from Spain, France or Morocco for an instantly lived-in look. These tiles can be used for the floor, work surfaces, behind the sink and even tabletops.

Bright, *inspiring, and lively*

Clean colors work well in a simple, stylized bathroom.

Bright aqua (**1**) is great for a bathroom. Use the yellow accent colors for ceramic or glass tiles on a strict, graphic, practical surface. Keep the look modern and simple since the bright colors need little decoration, and invest in quality chrome faucets and details.

1

2

3

Lemon foam (**3**) can be used for any woodwork in the room. Keep the lines straight and smooth and with a glossy finish.

Buttercup (**2**) can be used for the floor for a golden glow in the mornings. Choose this color for a neon-tinted-glass shower cubicle.

4

5

Keep the bathroom simple in plain white (**4**), but look for ultra-modern designs and sculpted, ergonomic shapes for the toilet, tub and sink.

Dark turquoise (**5**) is for the details. Have your favorite quote printed in vinyl lettering and run it around the walls for a quirky twist.

Delicate, *translucent twilight*

The clear and dainty tones of blue topaz (**1**) are like transparent colored glass, and can be used in a light, airy bedroom or bathroom. Choose translucent, floaty fabrics for the windows and tinted glass for any lamps, candleholders or even a chandelier. Layer colors in clever patterns and shades to create depth within the room.

Dreamy, glassy tints for a sanctuary at home.

This room is characterized by underplayed luxury. Nothing in here is ostentatious, but every surface suggests pure indulgence.

Choose celeriac (**2**) and sage (**3**) for chalky, flat painted surfaces around the room.

Slate blue (**4**) is perfect for upholstery in soft and tactile fabrics.

Choose lavender (**5**) for the few precious details that are on show in this room, such as heavy glass vases and oversized bowls filled with floating candles. Everything else should be cleverly hidden out of view.

Porcelain, *velvet and patterns*

This palette is inspired by vintage drawing rooms.

Forget-me-not (**1**) would be great in a period house with lots of original features. In a living room or dining area, a vintage-inspired wallpaper could be used on a single wall for a touch of decadent nostalgia. Choose a hand-blocked paper if possible for a truly original look.

1

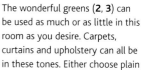

2

3

The wonderful greens (**2**, **3**) can be used as much or as little in this room as you desire. Carpets, curtains and upholstery can all be in these tones. Either choose plain woven fabrics, felted wool or low-sheen velvet. Opt for sofa-style armchairs with buttoned backs.

4

5

These colors will look equally dramatic whether in full daylight or in sultry candlelight. The levels of peach (**4**, **5**) bring a touch of light into this room. These colors are great as accents within patterning for wallpaper or decorative cushions. Choose pale-peach ceramics and source peach-tinted glass light fittings.

Streamlined *retro kitchenette*

Seawater (**1**) works well as a neutral backdrop. Here we have chosen classic beige and tobacco, traditional 1940s interior shades that are once more at the forefront of home-decorating styles. Choose furniture shapes reminiscent of the 1940s and 50s, and accessorize with bold, geometric-patterned fabrics and prints.

Mix modern with retro finds for an individual design.

Use this palette in a dining area or open-plan kitchen. Go for retro styling, such as a breakfast or cocktail bar in tobacco (**2**) with high stools in beige (**3**) and sliding-glass cupboard doors. Many interior companies are now making excellent reproductions of classic styles from this era.

Accessorize with cocktail glasses and a retro-style fridge, toaster and kettle in milkshake (**4**).

Source retro food packaging from the 40s and 50s in teal (**5**) and stack on shelves or countertops for a quirky touch.

Modern pattern, *graphic flowers*

A contemporary use of florals takes blue to the next level.

Aquamarine (**1**) is a lovely background shade – it gives a clean, bright finish without being overpowering. Today there are many fabric and wallpaper designers using patterns and floral imagery in a modern, graphic way. Look for styles of wallpaper that will inspire fresh palettes.

1

2

3

Use pale pistachio (**2**) for the woodwork. To make this space less feminine, keep details to a minimum and lines clean.

Fresh mint (**3**) can be used in patterns with bubble gum (**4**) and aniseed (**5**). You may need to use white as a background in some prints to break up the use of color.

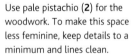

4

5

Bold, patterned upholstery is currently very popular, however, if you do not want to invest in pattern for all of the upholstery, then opt for plain aniseed. Accessorize with patterned cushions and curtains, and even patterned plates and cups.

Soothingly *neutral*

Sky blue (**1**) is brought down to a relaxing, tranquil environment with these tinted grays and warm neutrals. Create a completely serene atmosphere with underpowering shades. Nothing in this room should stand out too much. Everything is easy on the eye and everything has a place or a purpose.

An easy, tranquil mix of cool and warm hues.

Morning mist (**2**) is a wonderfully light and translucent color that would work well on both matte and glossy surfaces. Use this color for the woodwork.

Dove (**3**) can be used for soft furnishings. In a bedroom layer textures and textiles for a cozy night's sleep.

Warm neutrals (**4**, **5**) add a touch of luxury to the room. Choose suede for seat covers and soft sheepskin rugs for the floor. Source natural, carved blond-colored wood for bowls and candlesticks.

Chalky, *dusty powder*

Pale aqua is subdued with whitened shades of gray.

This palette utilizing pale cyan (**1**) is inspired by the horizon at dawn. At this time of day, colors are not overpowering – all are muted and each color blends happily into the next. That is how this room should seem: all colors are flat and easy on the eye creating a smooth transition from floor to ceiling.

Milky pink (**2**) is the color of yogurt; rich berry colors are flattened with the addition of dairy to create a softened tone. Use this color for soft furnishings in the room. Opt for felted-wool fabrics that reflect, rather than absorb, light to intensify the whitening effect.

Two levels of washed stone (**3**, **4**) are perfect for the woodwork and flooring. Again, opt for matte surfaces such as carpet or washed wood.

Raspberry bloom (**5**) is the strongest color, so use it for curtains and accessories.

Lifting *the room*

Lightness is key to many things in modern design: not simply with regards to color and weight, but also the uplifting, almost spiritual qualities that lightness provides. A light and airy room in ice blue (**1**) can change your mood and instantly make you feel less stressed and at ease.

Pale colors are a breath of fresh air in a dark, tired room.

1

2

3

Delicate shades like these can create a wonderfully relaxing and soothing environment. Many of us are wary of blue in the home since it can create a cold atmosphere. However, blue is said to provoke clear thinking and relieve the effects of insomnia, so use it in a study or bedroom.

4

Super-pale lemon (**2**) and pearl (**3**) can be used to paint the ceiling and the floor to exaggerate the expanse of space in a room.

5

The strongest shades of blue (**4**, **5**) can be used for woodwork, fresh linen on the bed and upholstery.

Provençal *lavender blue*

International colors inspired by country homes in France.

Blue is one of the most international of all shades. Many countries favor blue in their traditional housing and architecture. This palette of Provençal lavender blue (**1**) and soft pink is inspired by the country houses of Provence in France, with plaster walls and blue doors and window frames.

The main lavender blue can be used for the flooring and the ceiling since white is too harsh against these softened colors.

Soft pink (**2**) is the wall color. Try to find a natural, water- or lime-based paint for a rustic, matte finish. You could even mix the paint with a wash to create an aged finish on the walls.

French blue (**3**) is for the woodwork and door. Use the darker shade of ink (**5**) for painting kitchen cupboards.

Slate (**4**) can be used for heavy work surfaces and also for neutral furnishings.

Distinctive *and distinguished*

This cool blue (**1**) palette could either be used in a traditional setting for a living or dining area, or in a more modern, graphic way for a funky kitchen or den. The levels of light and dark can be used to create spaces within the room. If you have dark furniture, place it in front of a pale wall for maximum effect.

Individual colors that can be used to suit your taste.

1

2

3

The levels of green in this room are more yellow based, and bring warmth and light to the main cool blue (**1**). Greens and blues are a classic combination that can easily be used in a modern setting.

Soft avocado (**2**, **3**) colors are great for a kitchen. Use in tones on beveled kitchen doors – the darker shade creates a shadow.

4

5

Emerald (**4**) can be used for a striking tiled floor. Go for a resin-based, glossy finish for a stunning, jewel-like effect.

Black (**5**) can be used in Japanese-style serving plates and bowls, and polished granite work surfaces.

Country-*cabin chic*

A romantic palette of rustic browns and fresh blues.

This powder blue (**1**) palette is inspired by the wooden cabins of Scandinavia and Canada, old-fashioned homes that are becoming sought-after cottages for city dwellers. Exposed wood and brick, hand-carved furniture and traditional woven fabrics create a safe haven from modern life.

Powder blue (**1**) can be used for the flooring or to paint furniture. As much of this environment will be rich browns and natural wood surfaces, the blue acts as a fresh and contrasting color.

Use soft putty (**2**, **3**) colors to wash natural wood furniture.

This wonderful natural blue (**5**) would have been used in traditional woven fabrics and mixed with white. Source the traditional fabrics of the area for bedspreads, tablecloths and blankets.

Baby blue, *baby pink*

When decorating a room for children, baby blue (**1**) is traditionally used for a boy and pink for a girl. Today, the barriers are not so strict and you can mix the colors as you wish. Here we have a balanced mix of blues and pinks, and lights and darks that could be used for a child's or grown-up's bedroom.

A naive palette of colors not just for children.

1

2

3

Use soft dove gray (**2**) for the floor and woodwork. A gray shade in the color mix will prevent the room from becoming too sickly. Use gray in patterns within the room for cushions or bedspreads.

Stripes or checks in baby pink (**3**) and dove gray can be used to make loose covers for chairs and cushions.

4

5

Use raspberry cordial (**5**) and tutti-frutti (**4**) for fun details around the room. Why not hang a hammock instead of using conventional seating? Have several light fixtures put in the ceiling and hang different-shaped shades from them.

Wedgwood *and delftware details*

A palette inspired by 17th-century European ceramics.

A palette of china blue (**1**) is inspired by classic Wedgwood and delftware ceramics from England and Holland. The blue-and-white motifs of both designs are famous around the world. Advancements in the production of blues and greens in the 17th century made them favored interior colors of the era.

1

2

3

Originally invented by the Chinese and then copied by the Europeans, the blue glazes and patterns of Wedgwood and delftware have inspired design ever since. For a traditional look you could paint some of the naive scenes from the ceramics onto a wall. Alternatively, many hardware stores sell great imitation delft tiles that look fantastic in the kitchen, around the fireplace or in the bathroom.

4

5

Use a darker blue (**3**) to pick out features in a room.

The green levels (**4**, **5**) can be used for furnishing and carpets throughout the ground floor.

Violet, *pansy and blueberry*

Intense violet blues can be so strong that, even in nature, they look artificial – like on brightly-colored pansies, for example. Blues that occur in nature are a wonderful inspiration for the home. This shade of blueberry (**1**) has definite red undertones, which make it an easy, warm color to live with.

Warm violet colors encourage soft decorating in blue.

1

2

3

A symphony of gorgeous blue violets (**1**, **3**, **4**) are played off against each other. These tones can be used to highlight the architectural details in a room.

Use white (**2**) for the ceiling to lighten the mood. If you want a traditional chair rail, try striping white and blue violet below the rail.

4

Blushing pink (**5**) is a great counter color to the cooler violet shades. This injection of pink enhances the warmer quality of the blues and rounds off the mix. If you take away the pink, the palette becomes a single blur of shades of blue.

5

Regal *blue*

Take inspiration from the paintings of the old masters.

Historically, blues such as cornflower (**1**) were often used to represent royalty or religious figures. Ultramarine was made from a mineral called lapis lazuli, and it was more expensive than gold. The luxury and rarity of this color propelled it into the realms of wealth.

1

2

3

Combinations of blue, cream and brown are classic and can instantly create a luxurious environment. Use this palette for an aristocratic living room or library in the home.

Royal blue (**2**) can be used to paint the ceiling. For a very grand finish, paint tiny stars or have miniature bulbs set to create your very own constellation.

4

5

Use cream (**3**) for expensive leather seating and deep-pile plush carpeting.

Noisette and walnut (**4**, **5**) are perfect for the fireplace, small tables, heavy picture frames and leather-bound books.

Spiritual, *mysterious blue*

Blue, the color of the ocean and the sky on sunny days, always lifts the spirits and recharges your batteries. It represents space and freedom, and it is soothing and relaxing. All colors change the mood of a room, but blues such as hyacinth (**1**) can take you on any spiritual journey you desire.

A blue palette reflects a search for enlightenment.

Blues and greens, the colors of the natural landscape, always work well in interiors. Levels of light and dark will create a cocooned atmosphere. Darker colors help to keep out noise.

Spirit green (**2**) is a great color for window frames. Using green around the window helps to bring nature indoors.

Deep forest greens (**3**, **4**) can be used for the flooring and curtains. Choose low-level seating and rugs to lounge on.

Use ultramarine (**5**) for silk cushions, incense burners and blue glass lighting.

Casual *denim blue*

Get inspired by your wardrobe: use denim fabrics and fashion.

Denim (**1**) is no longer the reserve of students and cowboys; it is now seen as a quality fabric, used in luxury design for interiors as well as fashion. The hard-wearing quality of denim makes it a brilliant interior design solution. Choose from darkest indigo to pale stonewashed varieties.

Denim (**1**) is a flat color that needs lots of natural daylight and good accents to lift it.

Use dark denim (**2**) for seat covers in the kitchen, bathroom or den. For a funky dining area, cover chair seats with the fabric and use denim for napkins, too.

Stonewashed (**3**) can be used for the wood-work. This lighter shade of denim will help to marry all the colors in the scheme.

The mauve shades (**4**, **5**) will give warmth to the room. For a fun twist, use old T-shirts for cushion covers and lampshades.

Playful, *mischievous mix*

A clashing palette of bright bluebell (**1**) and reds will create a lively environment – colors do not always have to be in harmony in order to work. Primary colors such as blue and red always make a strong statement in an interior. Here, we use levels of light and dark colors to play tricks on the eye.

A fun mix of blues and reds for a funky bedroom interior.

Use large-scale graphic imagery on the bedcovers. You can even get personal photographs printed onto fabrics.

Use blueberry (**3**) for the carpet or flooring. Choose a flat material such as linoleum or rubber tiles.

Ink (**2**) can be used for the woodwork and to paint fine pinstripes on the walls in glossy paint.

Candy pink (**4**) and rouge (**5**) should be used in patterning or to paint details such as door handles and picture frames.

Bejeweled: *sapphire and emerald*

A precious palette of glossy surfaces and sparkling details.

Sapphire (**1**) is a rich, dazzling color which is intensified in glossy and metallic surfaces. In a dining or living area, paint a lacquer or varnish over the wall color to produce a glossy finish. This will reflect light into the room and saturate the colors further. Reinvent old furniture with glossy coats.

For decadent details use jewelry to adorn the walls. Collect costume jewelry from a second-hand store and pin brooches and necklaces to the wall in shapes and patterns.

Jet (**2**) can be used for the woodwork. Also use it for the tabletops or work surfaces. If you sand each coat of glossy paint and apply it carefully, a truly glossy finish can be achieved.

Emerald and jade (**4**, **5**) can be used for glass light shades. Mix emerald with a metallic glaze to paint mirror frames and the fireplace surround.

Rustic *farmhouse*

Rich dark blues have worked well with faded country stone reds and have been used all over Europe for centuries. This palette using French navy (**1**) takes inspiration from these simple yet effective color combinations for a great kitchen or any room that opens out onto a yard.

Country colors for interiors and exteriors.

Dark blue (**2**) is a richer shade of the French navy (**1**). Use this for the woodwork inside and out.

Find blue ceramic planters and dark wood (**3**) boxes to fill with dark-leaved foliage such as cordyline.

Use bark chips around the plants to discourage weeds from growing too quickly, and to give a constant hint of coloration.

Continue the theme from outside to indoors with red flagstone (**5**) floors and lots of surfaces in pale terra-cotta (**4**).

Mediterranean *island*

Inspired by white-washed houses and hot summer nights.

You may be inspired by the colors you find on your travels, but while rich, Mediterranean blue (**1**) and warm peaches look great in a sunny coastal village, they may not have the same effect in your home. Test colors on the walls before committing to a shade.

1

2

3

Traditionally, the villages of southern Spain, Greece, Italy and France are painted lime white to reflect the heat of the sun. Here we have chosen a warmer cream (**2**) that will be more cozy in an interior environment.

Hazy sky (**3**) can be used for the floorboards and window frames. Also, use it to paint mirrors or picture frames, and cupboards.

4

5

Peach and sunset orange (**4**, **5**) are hot, balmy colors that can be used in stripes or checks with the cream for fabrics. Choose hand-painted ceramics and bowls full of exotic fruits to finish the room.

Open *space*

Use paler colors for worktops in a kitchen to reflect the light. Rich ink (**1**) is lifted by a medley of paler tones. Deepest blue colors are deceiving in that they do not make the room appear smaller, but tend to open out a space and offer more light.

A simple blue and white palette gives a room a fresh feeling.

Choose scrubbed floorboards and simple wooden shutters at the window painted in buff (**2**). Why not hand paint folk-style patterns around the edge of doors and chairs? Leave woodwork clean and scrubbed.

For a more traditional look choose checked or polka-dot fabrics in pale gray (**3**) and air-force blue (**5**) for the seat covers, curtains and napkins.

Details can be kept basic with an old-fashioned butler's sink and white or pale gray ceramicware and crockery.

Violets

Blackberry, *cranberry and violet*

Blackberry violet is enlivened by flashes of cranberry.

Blackberry (**1**) is almost colorless, so it needs to be combined with some ambitious highlights to make the room inviting. Use this palette in a living or dining area for sumptuous relaxation. Tinted grays accentuate period features in a room, such as a grand fireplace, cornices or window shutters.

Storm-cloud-gray (**2**) and violet-gray (**3**) furniture can be inspired by the 1930s, with elongated, low chairs and even a deep-cranberry (**4**) chaise longue.

Choose velvets and satins in cranberry and peony (**5**) to give depth to these colors. Make sure the pale gray carpet is top quality and the curtains cascade to the floor. For a modern twist have cranberry-dyed sheepskins sewn together to create a huge rug.

Keep flowers in the room to stop the grays from being overbearing. Choose peonies or pink lilies for dramatic floral shapes to contrast with the violet walls.

Magical *and theatrical*

Dark grape (**1**) is one of the most sumptuous and decadent colors available in paints today. This rich and heady color has an aromatic quality, evoking images of ancient opium dens, lavish palaces and theatrical settings with over-the-top drapes and meticulous decoration.

A medley of violets for a decadent, decorated room.

Purple is not a color for everyone, however, when mixed with these dusty lavenders and chocolates, it is instantly irresistible.

Use the softened, dusky tones of dusty lavenders (**2**, **3**) for the woodwork, including armoires or chests of drawers in the bedroom.

Purple haze (**4**), the brightest of the colors, can be used for satin scatter cushions on the bed. Search for purple glass drawer handles, cocktail glasses or candlesticks.

Use bitter fig (**5**) for luxurious, satin quilted bedcovers.

Crocus, *lavender and lichen*

A luscious palette of rich, natural shades and floral tints.

Imperial purple (**1**) needs light colors to lift it, such as pale crocus (**3**) and soft iris (**2**). This palette can be altered to suit your personal preferences; if dark colors seem oppressive or the room you are working in is not very big, use pale crocus on one or two of the walls.

A completely purple room would be too much for most of us, so use a color like lichen (**4**) for the floor to lighten the mood.

Upholstery colors change depending on how many walls you choose to paint dark or light. In front of the pale crocus, choose bark (**5**), and in front of the dark purple choose pale crocus.

Soft iris (**2**) can be used for accessories such as lamp-shades, cushions and elaborate tassels to tie back the curtains, and for the tiles around the fireplace.

Garden *fresh*

Greens are often seen as a neutral shade since they complement all of the primary colors. Here we see just how good violets, like iris (**1**), and greens can look together. A combination taken straight from the garden is lightened and lifted into a pretty, yet modern bedroom or bathroom.

Violets and greens always complement each other.

Clear watery greens (**2**, **3**) are wonderfully light and refreshing colors that will lift the iris (**1**) shade. Use for glossy woodwork and bathroom fixtures. Bring lots of light into the room with multiple mirrors or a simple wall of mirrored glass above the bath.

Use dusty mauve (**5**) for the matte flooring.

Blue ripple (**4**) can be used for glassware in the bathroom or for candleholders for a relaxing bathtime. Use lavender oil and fresh cedar to complement the use of natural garden shades.

Storm-cloud violet, *new dawn*

Warmed, neutral shades sit happily on a mauve backdrop.

Yellow sits opposite purple on the color wheel. The cool and warm characteristics of the two shades complement each other and have become a classic mix in modern interior design. Storm cloud (**1**) takes inspiration from an overcast sky, with a streak of sunshine breaking through.

The main background color creates a perfect outline around pale straw and sunset colors. Choose matte linen in light straw (**3**) for the soft furnishings.

Sandstone (**2**) is a good color for stone, carpet or natural woven matting, such as sea grass or sisal.

Pink cloud (**4**) can be used for curtains and seat covers.

Use sunset orange (**5**) carefully and selectively with a couple of cushions placed on the sofa and a round vase of autumn roses on the mantel.

Opulent *and dramatic*

In the 1920s, after World War I, purple became a symbol of freedom. After years of grief and tension, wearing purple and using it in the home in colors like amethyst (**1**) seemed like a very extravagant thing to do. The color became synonymous with the flappers who danced all night and lived outrageously.

Jewel tones give a decadent, decorated feel to a room.

This rich yet lively group of colors will create real drama in any room in the house. The amethyst (**1**) walls need good lighting to lift them. Use this palette for a sexy, indulgent bathroom or for a theatrical dining room where the guests become the actors and the food is color coordinated.

Deep midnight (**2**) can be used for bathroom fixtures or dining furniture with a high-gloss finish.

Use bright, bold shades of turquoise (**4**, **5**) for glassware, and use candles and low lighting to bring the glass to life and allow it to sparkle around the room.

Scented *lavender*

*An aromatic palette
of garden blossoms
in full bloom.*

Cool lavender (**1**) and strong floral colors evoke images of romantic, hot summer evenings. This room should ideally open out onto a rose garden, but if you are not blessed with such a thing, then simply fill the window boxes with miniature roses and pungent lavender.

Imagine falling asleep with the soft scent of the garden floating in through the open window. Here, we capture that moment in color, and make it last through the winter months.

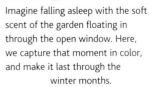

These pretty colors will lift the spirits on dark mornings. Use the pistachio (**2**) for translucent layers at the window and for a glass chandelier.

Antique green (**3**) can be used for the woodwork, crown molding and built-in cupboards. Have lots of mirrors in here, too, to bring in maximum light.

Rose pink (**4**) and scented stock (**5**) can be used to embroider white bed linen.

Smart, *stylish and classy*

This group of colors could decorate a luxurious living room or dining area. Mauve (**1**) is a wonderfully decadent shade within which to dine. This color will change dramatically with different lighting, offering a light, fresh lunch room and a rich and opulent evening space.

Violet colors work well in formal settings.

Choose fabrics, textures and surfaces carefully because quality is everything. Pale woods, such as pine and ash, can look expensive in the right setting. Use natural leather and suede tones (**2**, **3**) for napkins and place mats.

Silver always works well with violet shades, so invest in some silver napkin rings, and picture frames.

Regal purple (**4**) looks fantastic on deep-pile velvets for the curtains and dining-chair seats. Choose a patterned or textured velvet to exaggerate the depth of color.

Cool, *masculine loft living*

An urban palette for modern, open-plan bachelor lofts.

This quirky palette using violet gray (**1**) could bring life into a large space lacking focus. By using architectural details, such as pillars and joists, as features and sharp, acid flashes of color around the room, you can turn an empty shell into a modern, sophisticated environment.

1

2

3

Violet gray (**1**) and storm cloud gray (**4**) can be used to tint or paint the concrete surfaces in the space. Polished concrete is fast becoming a material of choice in many modern homes.

Pale aqua (**2**) is used to paint the remaining wall space in the area, encouraging calmness and tranquility.

4

5

Peacock (**3**) and glowing orange (**5**) can be used to draw the eye around the room. Use peacock for the kitchen area, on cabinets and work surfaces.

Graphite, *glass and neon*

Frosted lavender (**1**) is a great neutral shade: it is soft and unassuming, yet cool and warm, all at once. In open-plan environments such versatile colors are a must to use throughout. Then, create smaller spaces within the room through shapes and color use.

Architectural colors for open-plan, double-height arenas.

Paint the ceiling in pale sky (**2**) to artificially reduce the height of the room. For fun, you could even paint some clouds as a final touch.

Mid-blue (**3**) can be used for the doors, which could all be made from tinted glass to let in as much light as possible.

Dark teal (**4**) is a strong color that can be used to draw in an area. Paint a corner or a single wall with this color and use it as a backdrop for bitter lime (**5**) accessories. Treat your home like a gallery space, place neon-yellow glass pieces on shelves and spotlight them.

Iridescence *and sparkle*

Use delicate tinted pales for a fairy-tale room.

Be careful with very pale colors like lilac tint (**1**). Always test some paint on the wall first because even the softest shades can seem intense when used all over. Use fairy lights for magical evenings. By day, sunlight will catch on crystals and mirrors, sending sparkles around the room.

1

2

3

Lilac tint (**1**) can be enhanced by mixing it with pearlescent paint, making the walls literally shine.

Use flat, chalky surfaces in here too, so the room does not become too kitsch. Sweet candy floss (**2**) can be used for windowsills and baseboards.

4

Marshmallow (**3**) is a flatter tone that is perfect for flooring. Go for carpet or painted floor tiles.

5

Cowslip (**5**) is for the furnishings in soft suede or fluffy cashmere blends.

Sweet *and sugary*

Take inspiration from your favorite rich desserts with these mouthwatering colors. Paints and surfaces are good enough to eat in creamy, butter-soft leathers, colored-glass tabletops and shelves as pretty as hard candy. Delicate, sugared violet (**1**) is perfect for a pretty bedroom.

Peaches and cream, sugared violets and vanilla mousse.

1

2

3

Vanilla cream (**2**) and honey (**3**) are wonderfully soft and romantic pale shades. Use these tones for the ceiling and the floor. They will also mix perfectly with the main color in patterns and decoration. Choose faded miniature flower patterns for fabrics and wallpaper, and search out some vintage styles for a truly individual look. Many modern outlets supply whole ranges based on vintage and traditional designs.

4

5

Peach (**4**) and raspberry mousse (**5**) are delicious colors for details and assessories.

Considered *design*

A contemporary fusion of masculine and feminine style.

This room is modern yet sophisticated. Each area and accessory is well thought out and cleverly matched or placed. Dusty mauve (**1**) is an interesting color since such mid-tones are versatile, working in either a feminine or masculine way.

Dark rabbit-fur gray (**3**) is the main secondary color. Use it on woodwork and for sueded seats and sofas. This color works as a shadow shade to the main mauve.

Porcelain blue (**2**) can be used in a dining room for dishes and serving bowls; choose a high-gloss enameled finish if possible.

Musky rose (**4**) is a wonderfully deep color that would be great for heavy curtains and carpets throughout the downstairs areas of the house.

For a touch of glamor, add details in magenta (**5**), such as glass vases on the mantel and small cashmere cushions for the gray sofa.

Heather, amethyst, *mineral blue*

Heather (**1**) is tranquil and relaxing, creating an instantly homely and still environment in any room. For centuries many have believed that purple shades have magical powers that are both stimulating and soothing. Bearing this in mind, a room in this palette should be a haven in which to indulge the senses.

A calming bedroom environment to help you sleep.

Use dark heather (**3**) for the woodwork in the room.

Crystal blue (**2**) is an invigorating color, so paint the floorboards with it to lift the spirit of the room.

Dark amethyst and mineral blue (**4**, **5**) can be used to paint furniture such as chairs, bedside tables or an armoire.

This room can change with the seasons. In the warmer months stick to cotton bed covers in crystal blue and embroidered pillowcases. In the cooler times opt for layers of luxurious quilting on the bed and dyed sheepskin rugs on the floor for extra comfort and warmth.

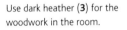

Sumptuous *indulgence*

Create a haven of luxury with clever colors and textures.

Dusty levels of mauve shades work well with natural colors. Black cherry mousse (**1**) is a wonderful shade to live with and brings warmth and a touch of glamor to the evenings and a liveliness to the day. Mid-tones are lifted by a clever use of accent shades and tactile surfaces.

1

2

3

Use natural gray (**2**) for the woodwork. In a space with traditional features, pick out the chair rail and ornate fireplace with rich eggplant (**5**).

Champagne (**3**) can be used for the flooring and for heavy, velvet curtains.

4

Eggplant really gives this room some drama. Use it in mixes for patterned cushions, dark picture frames and graphic shelving.

5

Light peach (**4**) is a pretty element. Use it for glass wall sconces that send dramatic patterns across the walls. Choose a pink-tinted mirror to hang above the fireplace.

Smooth, *diffused and mellow*

These colors may seem unspecific, but they are utterly beautiful and blend wonderfully from one to the next. Warm lavender (**1**) is the severest of the five shades, but clever use of the natural and greened tones will serve to dampen its intensity.

A sensitive blend of mid-tones creates a pleasing mood.

Neutral shades work very well with lavender since they warm the room and calm the intensity of the floral main color. Use stone (**2**) for the woodwork and for feather armchairs in soft wools or luxurious suede for total comfort.

Use straw (**3**) for natural sea grass woven matting.

Use cooler, greened neutrals (**4**, **5**) for cushions, heavy velvet curtains and misty layers of organdy at the windows. Find large enameled bowls for the table center and fill with succulent treats such as figs, cinnamon sweets or lavender-scented cake.

Cyclamen *and vivid pastels*

A pretty blend of colors brightens up a dull room.

Vivid cyclamen (**1**) needs softer tones to subdue its brightness. This palette is perfect for areas that do not get a lot of daylight. Intense shades can liven up windowless areas, such as a stairwell or hallway. Utilize the architectural shapes by painting surfaces in different colors.

1

2

3

If the main shade seems too intense, use pastel violet (**3**) and dusty heather (**2**) on alternate walls. These pretty colors would also be great for the ceiling in the stairwell to reflect maximum light.

Clear, crisp, minty greens (**4**, **5**) are perfect for a painted floor and any woodwork, including the front door and banister.

4

5

Feature your home's entrance with refreshing colors and quirky lighting. Why not invest in a modern, green-glass chandelier or light fixture to draw focus?

Graphic *Victorian decoration*

Victorian mauve (**1**) is a gorgeous color to use with the wallpaper and patterned fabrics that are making a comeback in modern interior design. Many companies produce ranges of wallpaper in contemporary and traditional styles. To ensure a pattern does not overpower the room cover only a single wall.

Introduce wallpaper with patterns and modern prints.

Violet and soft green (**3**) is a classic combination, favored by the Victorians in particular. This room needs bitter chocolate (**2**) for the woodwork as a graphic edge. Cover this dark shade with your hand on the page and see how instantly "pretty" the other colors are without its input. Choose a wallpaper with a linear quality that uses these contrasting shades.

The clear greens (**3**, **4**) are perfect for the fabrics in the room.

Choose the darker violet (**5**) for upholstery, or mix it with the bitter chocolate if the room looks too purple.

Mexican *colonial*

A soft violet gray enlivened with brick and rich indigo.

Inspired by Mexican painter Frida Kahlo's house, this palette using clay violet (**1**) is typical of a bohemian Mexican colonial dwelling. The rich indigo blue and earthy red have been copied throughout Mexico and beyond. Kahlo's use of color in her paintings was dramatic and bold, and this is reflected in her interior design.

Use earth red (**2**) for the flooring. Try a traditional rammed-earth floor, made from compacted earth and sealed with boiled linseed oil, which intensifies the color and gives a high shine.

Pale blue (**3**) and rich teal (**4**) can be used to paint geometric patterns onto cupboard doors in the kitchen. Find old paintings in second-hand stores with good use of color and hang them together on one wall.

Use deep indigo (**5**) for the woodwork and door. Continue this palette outside, since in hot countries living is undertaken both indoors and out.

1930s ocean-liner *glamor*

In this palette, colors are enhanced by the luxurious surfaces. Softest grays, shimmering velvets and deep-pile carpets all make for a decadent interior. Heliotrope (**1**) needs cool, neutral shades to help absorb the brightness of the color. Bold furniture is inspired by grand ocean liners with sweeping curves.

A decadent palette of elegant colors and cool shapes.

Silver and platinum (**2**, **3**) can be used for glossy details in the room. Paint the doors, window frame and the fireplace with these colors. Highlight details such as door handles, curtain rods and a fireplace with chrome or polished mirrored glass. Cover the top of a low, round table with mirrored glass and accessorize with cocktail glasses and pink champagne.

Striped platinum (**3**) and pink ice (**4**) can be used for the upholstery.

Use pale sea mist (**5**) for the flooring. For a grand approach, lay a pale wood parquet floor.

Windswept *and bracing*

Colors inspired by the beauty of a weathered seashore.

Nothing is more refreshing than a brisk walk along an exposed area of natural coastline. The unusual foliage and plant life in these areas are not seen elsewhere. On stormy days the sky, sea and land merge in waves of purple haze (**1**), creating a harsh and beautiful scene.

Bring these dramatic colors into the protection of your home for a harmonious palette. The main purple haze (**1**) is the color of deep storm clouds. Use it on the walls and see how everything else in the room stands out from this rich backdrop.

Sand and pebble (**2**, **3**) are perfect colors for the woodwork. In a bathroom choose natural pebble flooring for a great massage underfoot.

Choose ice blue (**4**) and bleak gray (**5**) for large furniture and the pieces will look amazing framed against the purple. Choose wool fabrics for a soft, whitened finish.

Ripe, *juicy plum*

Plum (**1**) is decadent and full – a passionate color not for the fainthearted. Use strong colors like these in a cozy den or a sexy bedroom. Mix these ripened colors with sumptuous surfaces. Choose smooth satin for the bed and soft carpet for the floor. Soft lighting will enhance the deep shades.

Rich, berry tones always produce an extravagant room.

Softer, milkshake pinks (**2**, **3**) can be used for the woodwork and the furniture, such as a chest of drawers, armoire or sideboard. Use lots of mirrors to bring in maximum light.

Highlights of forest fruits, like blackberry (**4**) and blueberry (**5**), really give depth to this luscious environment. Do not be afraid of such dark colors: use them with confidence and the end result will always be successful. Cover old armchairs in deepest-berry velvets for total indulgence. These mouthwatering tones will enhance the plum tone of the walls without being overpowering.

Art deco *outlining*

A graphic black outline underscores these stylized pinks.

Look to the art deco period of the 1930s, an era in design characterized by geometric shapes, clean lines and simple use of color, for a dramatic finish. Blackcurrant (**1**) is lifted with cool pinks and a silvery green. Create a dramatic entrance to your home using these colors.

Cool pink (**3**) can be used in recesses or alcoves to flood light into that area. Use black (**2**) to outline shapes in the room. Woodwork, stair rails and crown molding can all be black. For a truly decadent look, go for a glossy black floor; it will reflect the color in the room.

Hot pink (**4**) is for some giant ostrich feathers to stand in a glossy, black vase in the corner of the room.

Use silver gray (**5**) for the furniture. Paint pieces this color and outline cupboard doors and drawer handles in black.

Bohemian *eggplant*

This is a wonderful palette of rich, sexy darks and vibrant, modern brights. Eggplant (**1**) has become a very popular interior shade. Many contemporary bars and restaurants use a similar tone to create an instantly warm and cozy environment.

Eccentric, rich colors for a truly original setting.

Deep eggplant (**1**) makes a fabulous wall-covering, intense and sultry. Use a varnish or gloss over the color to intensify the richness.

Chocolate (**3**) is for the dark, exotic furniture in the room. An intricate, carved wooden door from the Far East can be topped with glass and made into a table.

Lavender, orange-bloom and bright tangerine (**2**, **4**, **5**) can be used to create unusual dinner settings with hand-painted dishes and colored glassware.

All colors can be mixed together in intricate Persian rugs to cover the floor and some of the walls.

Neutrals

Timeless *quality*

A traditional palette with a twist.

A dark, grayed neutral can be a cozy color. Mix bark (**1**) with softened dusky pinks, old-fashioned red and soft sand for instantly comfortable surroundings. This palette offers soothing background tones and modern accents, making it an easy color scheme to get right.

Choose comfortable, soft furnishings for a room that you can truly relax in. The mix of dark and light colors makes it an equally great place to be in the daytime or in the evening with soft candlelight.

Use soft pinks (**2**, **3**) for patterned rugs on the floors. The darker shade is for heavy, woven curtains.

Faded red (**4**) can be used to cover small pieces of furniture, such as a footstool or nested tables.

Sand (**5**) is a lovely, rich yellowed neutral, great for tiling around a fireplace.

Room *to contemplate*

Soft mink (**1**) is cocooning and protective. Wrap yourself in these warming, fall shades for a quiet place to read and think, away from the hustle and bustle of the city. Houses today can be busy and noisy, so it is very important to find an area within the home that is peaceful and private where you can relax.

Soft yet invigorating colors for a quiet reading area.

Invest in a designer chair and have it covered in a graphic, 1950s-style fabric to make a centerpiece. Although the colors are flat, you can experiment with the details in this room. Remember, this is your own private space so do whatever you want.

Keep large pieces of furniture pale and simple for a restful atmosphere. Use warm white (**2**) for the floor and the ceiling. Keep the window bare to let in the maximum amount of light.

Rusted oranges (**4**, **5**) can be used for a fun retro reading lamp and a cozy checked blanket.

Rose-tinted *romantic*

A discreet, sentimental palette of natural shades.

Natural string (**1**) is an uncomplicated, easy background color. You can create almost any design with this tone as a base. Such colors are reminiscent of a simpler way of life, not driven by the industrial age. Coordinate this palette with natural surfaces and fabrics.

In a bathroom use natural stone with a sandy quality for the bathtub and sink. The same stone can be used to cover the floor. Alternatively, opt for dark wood floorboards.

Dusky rose (**3**) and madder red (**4**) can be created from natural dyes. Bring some much needed color into this room with bowls of dried rose petals.

Use unbleached natural linen (**5**) and organic cotton for towels and curtains. There is no plastic or man-made material in this room. All ointments and cosmetics are made from natural, organic ingredients and stored in glass jars with hand-written labels.

Oyster *shell*

Use rich oyster (**1**) in a bedroom or bathroom for a soft, relaxing mood. You could mix this color with an iridescent or sparkle medium to create a stunning, subtle shimmer on the walls. By day this would light up the room and by night, flickering candles will illuminate the sparkles.

This low-level palette features exaggerated natural tones.

The accent tones in this palette are intensified, pearlescent colors. Cool and pretty, these shades would work well mixed in patterns or as flat, solid expanses.

In a bedroom use soft gray blue (**3**) for the woodwork, and paint the bedside tables to match.

Use delicate mint (**2**) for glassware and lighting. In the bathroom fit a glass shower cubicle in this color.

Use heather (**4**) and pink (**5**) for the bedcovers. Choose a delicately beaded or embroidered throw for an embellished touch.

Jungle *camouflage*

Create a fun indoor play area for children.

Bring the outdoors in with an extreme playroom for all the kids using sand (**1**). Use ropes and camouflage netting to section off areas of the room and put rubber tiles on the floor for protection. Fit climbing rings to the walls and hang hammocks up instead of using chairs.

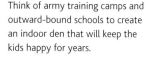

Think of army training camps and outward-bound schools to create an indoor den that will keep the kids happy for years.

Use natural sand colors (**1**, **2**) for the walls. Paint the darker color up to halfway and the lighter color up to the ceiling.

Use khaki (**3**) for the flooring, either rubber or scuff-proof linoleum.

Rich browns (**4**, **5**) can be used for the fun elements in the room. Paint the children's names graffiti-style across the wall and have a wipe-clean area especially for finger painting.

For the truly daring, why not put a sandbox in the middle of the floor?

Straw, *wheat and corn*

A palette inspired by countryside colors can work equally well in a city dwelling. If you want to bring a touch of the real and the rustic to a modern apartment, then look no further than this straw (**1**) shade. Reminiscent of sun-scorched afternoons on country roads, these tones will give a boost to any tired area.

Ripening fields inspire yellowed neutrals.

This color palette could easily be utilized throughout the ground floor of a home or within an open-plan environment. Soft, cream walls can easily move from the kitchen to the living area to the dining room.

Use red earth (**2**) tiles for the flooring. In an area where you want more warmth, such as the den, place a large, patterned rug in natural ocher (**3**) shades by the hearth.

Summer green (**4**) can be used for cupboard doors and upholstery.

Use pretty touches of peach (**5**) in watercolor pictures and ceramics.

Discreet, *considerate, reserved*

The most colorless of palettes can often be the most striking.

It sometimes takes more courage to leave things out of a design than to put things in. Milk (**1**) needs simple themes and uncluttered rooms to make for a very rewarding interior design. If you can live simply and hide away your clutter, then this clean, elegant color is for you.

1

2

3

Mix and match these harmonious shades of pale in any form you like. If you want a darker emphasis in the room then simply make the burlap (**5**) highlight color your major secondary color, perhaps in the form of scrubbed wooden surfaces.

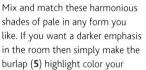

4

5

Natural materials would work best in here, such as a limestone floor that emulates all the tones in the palette.

Stack creamy ceramic plates on open wooden shelves. Remove all food from its packaging and put into tin or glass containers for a uniform finish.

Buttermilk *and olive*

Buttermilk (**1**) is a gently warmed neutral. This type of color will create a soft yet sophisticated background. Choose natural linen and woven fabrics for this room, and opt for naturally dyed surfaces if at all possible. You could even try covering parts of the walls in fabric; panels give the best result.

Mix warm neutrals and olive green for elegant dining.

Green is said to behave just like a neutral. Stone and flat green (**2**, **3**) can be used as the background shades, perhaps on the flooring and woodwork in the room. You could keep the mix simple, or use these colors in a pattern of psychedelic swirls for retro accessories, such as storage boxes, cushions, or seat covers.

Use rich olive (**4**) and lime (**5**) in shocking glassware, or collect vintage, patterned Bakelite cups and saucers to display.

Tropical, *exotic palm house*

A palette inspired by the palm greenhouses of the 1920s.

A whitened, ivory (**1**) -colored, sun-filled room filled with exotic plants, such as palms, orchids and ferns, creates an indoor garden in a sunny living room or kitchen. Take reference from traditional palm houses with ornate windows, French doors and large, plant-filled pots.

Use pebble (**2**) for the tiled flooring. For a high-tech twist invest in underfloor heating to keep a tropical temperature all year round.

Use levels of green for a calming, tranquil atmosphere. Softened fern (**3**) is a great color for the woodwork and for the plant pots in the room.

Mix green leaf (**4**) and orchid (**5**) with white in exotic floral prints for cushions and curtains or shades. Match paint to real flower colors for a special twist.

Choose wicker furniture and glass tabletops.

Latte, *espresso and cappuccino*

This decadent palette of caffé latte (**1**) browns and neutrals could easily be inspired by an expensive restaurant or coffee shop interior. These simple tones work well together to create a neutral yet luxurious background. This color mix would work well in the kitchen, living room or dining area.

A frothy mix of creams and aromatic coffee colors.

A simple, classic mix of colors for creating a stylish atmosphere.

Use café au lait (**2**), a subtle shade darker than the main color, for the woodwork.

Use coffee bean (**4**) for an area of the room, such as a chimney breast, or pick out features such as beams or alcoves. Offset this dramatic dark color with framed black-and-white photography on the pale wall in the room.

Use cream (**5**) for fluffy sheepskin cushions and a cashmere throw on the brown leather (**3**) sofa.

Golden, *filtered sunlight*

A sun-filled palette brings cheer and warmth to the home.

Use levels of golden yellow and papyrus (**1**) to mimic the effect of the sun being filtered through the shades into the room. These tones are great neutral colors for a guest room that may not get used as often as other rooms, or use them in a kitchen, bathroom or bedroom. Such a palette has wide appeal.

1

2

3

Lemon mousse (**2**) can be used for the bed linens. Stripe it with lemon butter (**3**) for the duvet cover and chair covers.

Use bright gold (**4**) for hand-painted details around the door and windows. There are many stencil companies that offer quick and easy patterns and flowers to adorn the walls.

4

5

Hen's egg (**5**) can be used to paint wooden furniture, such as an old-fashioned school chair and a simple table with a drawer.

Place a vase of daisies on the table whenever there are guests using the room.

African *adobe*

This palette takes its references from traditional African dwellings, clay (**1**), adobe houses and naturally dyed yarns used to weave indigenous fabrics. If you find a piece of fabric at home or abroad that you simply love, why not create a whole room around that one item?

Earthy hues that can be cleverly mixed for the modern home.

If you can source it, use natural distemper or limewash on the walls for a flat, simple finish. Adobe, or dried earth, is used in one-third of the housing in the world today. This ancient but beautiful finish is being revived by modern architects.

Use African carved wood for the furniture. In large towns you can find an importer of exotic furniture or check online – just beware of shoddy imitations.

Rich Persian red (**5**) and adobe (**4**) can be mixed with the main color in traditional woven fabrics to drape over furniture and walls.

Bold *color blocking*

Soft beige is enlivened with jewel-colored accents.

This is a classic 1960s palette of biscuit (**1**) shades, intense greens and turquoises. You can still find objects such as mugs, teapots and storage tins in the original, swirling, psychedelic patterns. Use these sparingly and focus on using clever blocks of color.

1

2

3

This palette could easily work in an open-plan environment, since the soft colors (**1**, **2**, **3**) can be used to split areas of the room to denote kitchen, living room and bedroom while the stronger colors (**4**, **5**) can be used to segregate with bold painted stripes.

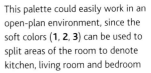

Keep the floor pale throughout in willow (**3**) for a light effect.

4

5

Use the stronger colors such as cactus (**4**) and teal (**5**), to create blocks of color on the walls and around the room with one-off pieces of furniture and colored window shades that stand out against the paler colors.

Stone, *rose quartz and amethyst*

Stone (**1**) sounds like a cold color, but there are many types of stone that can be used in the home. Choose a yellow- or red-based stone, such as limestone, for a warm feeling. This natural material can be used throughout a bathroom or kitchen for the floor, the surfaces and the tiling.

A palette of natural mineral tones can be pretty and feminine.

Pale stones are nearly always mixed with light or neutral colors. Mix with pretty levels of rose quartz and amethyst for a stronger use of color.

Rose quartz (**3**) can be used for all of the remaining walls.

Use pretty tones of amethyst (**4**, **5**) for towels, soaps and chair covers.

Accessorize the bathroom with natural lumps of crystal and amethyst, which will look stunning against the stone. Direct lighting toward them, or light with candles for maximum effect.

A garden room *with lavender*

Fill a room that opens to the outdoors with floral shades.

This palette is perfect in a room that opens out onto a garden. If one entire wall opens out into the garden then the definition between inside and out can be pleasantly blurred. Since the area should be filled with plants, this palette uses muted oatmeal (**1**) as a very subtle backdrop.

Use natural stone paving slabs on the floor, and run a water channel around the edge of the room to irrigate the plants.

Use muted oatmeal (**1**) for walls, or mix it with white and pale lavender (**3**) for a striped, hand-painted finish. Alternatively, mix these colors in checked or polka-dot fabrics to cover the chairs.

Use garden lilac and purple (**4**, **5**) for plant pots. Mix with galvanized steel if you want a more industrial feel.

Business-like *and smart*

As many more of us are working from home, we need areas within the house suitable for meeting clients or holding meetings. Home-office environments do not need to be as formal as the real thing, but create an air of professionalism with smart olive (**1**) colors.

Shades of tailored neutrals create a chic working area.

Take references from a good tailor: use only the best-quality materials and make sure everything in this room fits properly. With clever storage and classy furniture, the office can quickly be packed away to create a stylish dining area.

Soft green (**2**) and faded charcoal (**3**) should be used for glass worktops and carpeting for a relaxing, tranquil atmosphere.

For a slick finish, choose pinstriped fabrics or tweeds in deep gray (**4**) for the chair covers.

Dark navy (**5**) can be used for seamless cupboard doors that open with just a touch.

Embellished, *Indian exotic*

A richly decorated room based on India's palaces.

Once upon a time, the Taj Mahal was decorated with real jewels. Rubies and emeralds that sparkled in the sunshine were carefully embedded into the walls of the palace. Build a highly decorated room reminiscent of the elaborate palaces of India by using a base color of dust (**1**).

1

2

3

Use darkest emerald (**5**) for the woodwork and a heavily framed mirror.

Use beaded sari fabrics for curtains and cushion covers. Every surface in this room can be covered in some kind of rich ornamentation.

4

Faded red and deep ruby (**3**, **4**) can be used for patterned upholstery. Choose traditional paisleys.

5

Hang colored glass lanterns from the ceiling to cast pretty patterns around the room.

Deep khaki, *cobalt and black*

Deep khaki (**1**) needs bright, uplifting colors to stop it from appearing drab. Violet blue (**3**) and cobalt (**4**) are great, strong pigment colors that really shine when used in any environment. Use geometric patterning, either in an area of wallpaper behind the dining table or even as a feature atop the table itself.

A graphic palette of dark and light shades.

This modern color palette could create a dramatic effect in a dining room. Use black (**2**) for the woodwork, including the doors and crown molding. Black is making a dramatic comeback as the woodwork color of choice in modern interior design.

Use palest blue (**5**) for tinted-glass shelving. Place cobalt (**4**) glasses and ornaments on the glass shelf, light it from below and admire the graphic shapes created on the walls.

Grays

Cool, *clean and contemporary*

A great, modern palette for a stylish kitchen environment.

Granite (**1**) is dark enough to offer warmth. Combine it with cool grays and blues to create an instantly stylish area, perhaps a totally high-tech kitchen. Choose stainless steel appliances and spend a little extra on the details, such as designer faucets, light switches and door handles.

1

2

3

Ice (**2**) and aluminum (**3**) are perfect for contemporary kitchen units. Choose ice-tinted glass for the work surfaces for a clean style. Lighting is very important in the kitchen – always have good, directional lighting, such as spotlights, around the work surfaces.

4

5

Check out some of the modern, resin floor tiles currently available. Glass-effect floor tiles can give a room a light and modern feeling instantly.

Slate blue and deep ocean (**4**, **5**) can be used for window shades, seat covers, and serving bowls. Add splashes of color around the room.

Sunshine *bright*

Concrete (**1**) and yellow are a good combination. With cool levels, warm shades and darker tones, you can play with shadow and light here. In a kitchen, think carefully about where the sun comes in the morning so your breakfast area is assured a sunny wake-up.

Flat gray enlivened with a burst of sunshine yellow.

Yellow is a common color to use in the kitchen. By combining it with gray shades, you can create a modern design rather than the usual country-kitchen look.

Choose pale ash (**2**) for the cupboard doors and chrome for handles and appliances.

Rich cream and lemon (**3**, **4**) can be used for plates, cups and serving bowls. Go for a lemon worktop for a refreshing change.

Sunshine (**5**) is a strong color and should be used sparingly. Paint the back-door panels and cover the chair seats with it, striped with gray if you prefer.

Warm *and harmonious*

Bright turquoise livens up a medley of neutral shades.

Neutral tones always look good layered on top of each other. Natural sand and stone colors can be used in almost any combination for a soft, cozy, comfortable environment. Here, pebble (**1**) is enhanced with warming natural shades. The contrasting turquoise gives a modern kick.

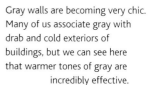

Gray walls are becoming very chic. Many of us associate gray with drab and cold exteriors of buildings, but we can see here that warmer tones of gray are incredibly effective.

Use blonde and pale wood (**2**, **3**) for the flooring and the window and door frames since they will lift the gray.

Chocolate and turquoise (**4**, **5**) are a classic design combination. Use brown leather for furniture and picture frames. Accessorize with a turquoise cashmere blanket and a turquoise telephone. Stand a large rock of real turquoise on the mantel as a feature.

Lichen, *sage and willow*

Tinted neutrals form a highly sophisticated level of colors. The soft tones of lichen (**1**) colored with green or pink create a subtle glow, and change dramatically depending on whether the light is natural or artificial. Neutrals are the perfect blank canvas upon which to paint the picture of your interior design.

Green-tinted gray makes a natural backdrop.

Sage (**3**) is a stunning level of green to live with. It is natural, pretty and relaxing all at once. You could use sage to paint floorboards or kitchen or bathroom cabinets, or use it for a luxurious carpet in a bedroom or living room.

Willow (**2**) is a fairly bright green and can be used on floor-length curtains or for any woodwork .

Lime white (**4**) brings light to this room. Paint the ceiling and the floor with it for maximum reflection in the room.

Rose (**5**) brings a touch of prettiness. Fill a vase with pink blooms such as peonies.

Precious *metal*

An indulgent palette of pales for a salon-style interior.

This palette is rather impractical for many homes. Soft, tinted layers of whites and silver gray (**1**) would not last long in a family environment. However, if you are looking for a style statement, there can be little more classy than this sophisticated level of precious metals.

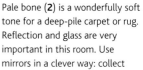

Pale bone (**2**) is a wonderfully soft tone for a deep-pile carpet or rug. Reflection and glass are very important in this room. Use mirrors in a clever way: collect antique beveled-edge mirrors and cover a single wall with them to bring maximum light into a dark room.

Use darker gray (**3**) for the woodwork and furnishings as a graphic edge. Find 1930s-style curved chairs, and maybe a chaise longue, and cover them with shimmering silk velvet.

Light ceramic (**4**) and dusk (**5**) can be used to make layers of diaphanous drapes at the windows.

Weathered *and seashore fresh*

Lead white (**1**) is reminiscent of the colors of wooden houses by the seashore. The salt air and harsh, coastal breezes break down paint and give surfaces a wonderful, natural matte, sandblasted finish. Coastal living has its own design ethos, which can be recreated in any building, even in the city.

A palette of sea-foam colors, scrubbed and washed by sea air.

Lead white (**1**) is perfectly complemented by a medley of sea greens and weatherboard blues. Choose wooden surfaces where possible. Flat paint is best: it can be watered down and used as a thin, light wash on wood to achieve an instantly weathered look.

Use sea foam (**2**) to paint wooden floorboards or for a simple linoleum flooring. Sky (**3**) is a great neutral color to choose for bathroom fixtures or for kitchen cupboards.

Sea heather (**4**) and thistle (**5**) can be used for solid, handmade earthenware plates and bowls.

Glowing *accents*

With colored accents you can easily change your interior

For a totally versatile interior choose ash (**1**) for the walls and simply build your design onto this blank page. By choosing brighter colors for the accents and highlights, it is easy and economical to change the look of the room when you feel like something new.

1

2

3

These four levels of pink range from softest ballet slipper (**2**) to rich raspberry (**5**). Mix the colors in fine-striped or polka-dot fabrics to cover chairs and a sofa.

4

5

Whitened rooms can look fantastic with lots of colorful accessories. Paint shelves and tables in geranium (**4**), or light surfaces from beneath with pink strip lights.

Position colored fairy lights in any of the pink shades in dark corners of the room. These wonderful pink tones will positively glow against the whitened walls.

Subtle *tints*

Tinted whites have always been popular interior colors. It is quite amazing what a difference such a subtle tint of color can make. Choose creamy vanilla (**1**). The accent colors of honey and cinnamon will be reflected in the white paint, perfectly complementing this tint.

A perfect palette for a welcoming kitchen nook.

Linen (**2**) is a great shade, not too bright, but balmy and sunny enough to bring some cheer into any room. Use it for upholstery and curtains.

String (**3**) is a neutral shade but has a warming, pink undertone to keep the room cozy. Use it on the work surfaces and kitchen cupboards.

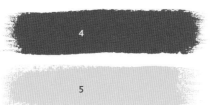

Cinnamon (**4**) is a great kitchen color. Use it in a rustic style with terra-cotta tiles on the floor, and Mediterranean-style handmade bowls and plates. For something more modern, mix it with a metallic decorative finish for copper detail on the woodwork.

Powdered *cosmetics*

*Take inspiration
from cosmetic colors
for a girly bedroom.*

Marble (**1**) is the delicate foundation color for this room. Build the look on top of it with fragile layers of rouge and shimmering eye-shadow pinks. To complete the look, accessorize with lipstick shades of deep plum on shiny glass vases and polished tabletops.

These pinked levels are flattering and sensitive. In a bedroom, choose shades that are delicate or softened with white for a more subtle approach.

Choose simple shapes of furniture. Mix the eye-shadow pinks (**2**, **3**) with a very subtle pearlescent decorative finish to cover the bedside tables, drawers and armoire.

Dusty lilac (**4**) can be used for the flooring and bed linens.

Finish off the room with accents of plum (**5**). Use it for super-glossy woodwork, and paint the bed frame for a glamorous touch.

Playful *naivete*

This is a room of contrasts: silver fox (**1**) is brought to life with bright, sunny pigments. This palette is suited to a room with maximum natural light which will enhance the freshness of the bright colors. Choose shiny, modern surfaces, such as molded plastic seating.

Mix cheerful tones of blue and yellow with a tranquil gray.

1

3

Silver fox (**1**) makes for a flat, blanketed foundation. Cover all of the walls and the floor with this color and simply use the remaining colors to pick out details in the room.

Use frozen blue (**2**) on the ceiling for a lightened, airy feeling.

4

Summer sky (**3**) can be used for the woodwork. The naive use of primary colors will give this room a childlike, almost dollhouse, quality.

5

In a bathroom, mix and match the accessories in blue and yellow (**4**, **5**) for a playful theme.

Dusk, *half light, sundown*

Delicate sunset shades reflect light around a room.

As the sun is setting, a strange half-light occurs no matter where you are. It casts unusual shadows and reflects strange colors around an interior. It is an exceptionally beautiful moment in time. With dusk (**1**) and these shades of sunset pink, we try to capture that moment.

1

2

3

Use these colors in a room that catches the evening light. In summer, this light will naturally heat up the room and give a glow to everything within.

Dusk (**1**), a pretty, soft gray, is warmed with tints of sunset pink (**3**, **4**) and bold, burning orange (**5**).

4

Use dove gray (**2**) for a feather-filled sofa in velvet or suede. Cover the sofa with scatter cushions in all shades of pink and orange.

5

On the gray walls, hang orange-tinted glass lamps that reflect around the room and continue to warm the environment long after sunset.

Turning *leaves*

In nature, as winter approaches the light becomes less bright and the trees change color from green to russets and browns. Rich colors like cashmere (**1**) have inspired painters for centuries. Take note of the seasons and be inspired by the new colors that each has to offer.

Flattened fall shades can be rich and inviting.

These colors could make a wonderful kitchen or dining area. With cashmere on the walls, paint the cupboards and cabinets a richer level of mocha (**2**).

Choose russet (**3**) for the work surfaces and tiling.

Go for a dark, stained wood floor for a more cozy atmosphere. Bitter chocolate (**5**) is a rich and warming color. If you have an open fire, source a dramatic mantel and stain it in this dark color.

Peach (**4**) can be mixed with russet and chocolate in checked fabrics for seat covers and curtains.

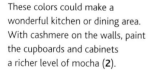

Fake *furs*

A design inspired by fake-fur throws is utterly indulgent.

Today, fake fur is so good that we have no need for the real thing. Throws, bedcovers and rugs in rabbit fur (**1**) and dyed sheepskin have become an integral part of interior design. Why not layer fur around the room, like in the bedroom of a Russian princess?

Even fake fur has a wonderful, shimmering, soft quality to it, with several shades and colors apparent in every piece. Use subtle levels of mink and gray (**2**) in a bedroom to emulate the colors in the fur bed throw.

Use dusty heather (**3**) for the woodwork and a painted floor for a pretty, but still cool, edge.

Dye some sheepskins in deep purple (**5**) and have them on the floor around the bed.

Use feathers dyed mauve (**4**) to trim the lampshade and the edge of cushions to continue the textural theme.

Winter gray *and iced mint*

Fresh, cool mint and dove (**1**) make a wonderful partnership. This color scheme works well in a bathroom or a modern, streamlined kitchen. Choose easy-to-clean, waterproof surfaces, such as tiles and paint with an antifungal treatment to prevent mildew; the crisp colors will stay fresher for longer.

A refreshing palette of icy mints and cool grays.

With the main warmed mid-gray on the walls, the delicate shades of green and mint will be able to take over the room.

Use smoky ice (**2**) for the woodwork and flooring. Opt for something with a flawless finish such as linoleum or bonded rubber tiles.

The three shades of mint (**3**, **4**, **5**) can be used in varying degrees. Use the palest shade for the larger furniture, such as the bathroom fixtures or cupboard doors in the kitchen. Use green-tinted glass for the shower doors and counters.

Timeless *desert detailing*

Classic layers of grays and natural, sandblasted shades.

Natural shades used in interiors often evoke an uncomplicated, unchallenging atmosphere. The colors in this palette are synonymous with a simpler way of life. Even in a city apartment, mineral gray (**1**) can create an unpretentious environment.

1

2

3

Nothing in this room is flashy or ostentatious. Simple pleasures of cooking, eating and spending time with friends and family are the backbone of this room.

4

5

The oven and a large wooden table are the focus. Color wash the scrubbed wooden surfaces with pebble (**3**) for a lighter finish.

Choose natural slate for the floor, but invest in underfloor heating to warm up the room.

Warm terra-cotta colors (**4**, **5**) can be used for rustic earthenware serving bowls and tactile, handmade mugs.

A neon *lift*

There is an infinite variety of gray shades. You can easily tint basic grays with warmer or cooler shades to complement the other colors in your palette. A flagstone gray (**1**) is the perfect backdrop color. The soft, dusty shades are lifted with a clever use of neon brights.

Gray makes the perfect backdrop to bold, garish brights.

Muted gray (**2**) can be used for the woodwork. Create artificial panels on the walls with wooden beading and fill them with this plaster color for a traditional, paneled-room look.

Within these panels you can frame pieces of furniture or accessories. Cover a single chair with neon pink (**4**) velvet and place it against the gray backdrop on one side of the room. On the opposite side, place the same chair covered in gray fabric against a plaster backdrop and accessorize with a neon yellow (**5**) cushion. Place alternate pink and yellow single vases along the mantel.

Titanium *and stainless steel*

Choose architectural finishes for a cool, modern kitchen.

Take inspiration from the American architect Frank Gehry and his design for the Guggenheim Museum in Bilbao, Spain. Vast, curving expanses of polished metal panels look dramatic and give a clean, hi-tech finish. Choose steel (**1**) for walls and metal sheeting for cabinets.

Utilize the natural quality of stainless-steel surfaces with their dulled, polished finish. This reflects color, but is not too shiny or overpowering.

Pale silver (**2**) can be used for high-gloss flooring. Use either polished concrete or glass-effect resin tiles.

Use cool blue (**3**) tones to complement the amount of gray in the room, and choose bright-blue (**4**) tinted glass for the work surfaces.

Dark navy (**5**) can be used for seat covers. For a classy finish, why not choose navy pinstriped suiting fabrics or a smooth wool flannel?

Credits

Quarto would like to thank and acknowledge the following for supplying photographs reproduced in this book:

2 David George www.david-george.co.uk
9 Sukey Parnell
11 Eric Roth / Susan Sargent Design
www.ericrothphoto.com www.susansargent.com
12 Botanica / Getty Images
16 Sukey Parnell
18 Tim Imrie / Abode
20 Stephen J.Whitehorne / Myriad Images
21 Jan Baldwin / Narratives
22 Bonga Design – contemporary lighting for
the domestic & commercial market
www.bongadesignlighting.co.uk
23 Gareth Brown / Corbis

24 David George www.david-george.co.uk
28, 29, 30, 31 Sukey Parnell
36, 60, 80, 106 Jan Baldwin / Narratives
132, 158, 188 David George
www.david-george.co.uk
214 Jan Baldwin / Narratives
234 Lindsey Stock / Myriad Images

All other illustrations and photographs are the copyright of Quarto Publishing plc. While every effort has been made to credit contributors, Quarto would like to apologize should there have been any omissions or errors, and would be pleased to make the appropriate correction for future editions of the book.

Acknowledgments

I must thank a few people, without whom, this book would never have become anything more than a never-ending mountain of color references and painted swatches.

Firstly, thank you to the lovely folk at Quarto for having the faith in me to put this thing together, for putting up with my perfectionist tendencies and for allowing me to learn from them, especially Kate, Moira and Penny. Thank you to Anna and Claudia for their patience in picture research and to Stephen for sorting out problems in a very gentlemanly fashion. A very special thank you to Trisha Telep for her boundless enthusiasm and energy, and for her illicit midnight copy drops! Thanks to Sukey Parnell for her willingness to shoot some extra (gorgeous) pictures, and for her continued good advice and creative support. I would like to dedicate this book to Iain, who has taught me to see the beauty in every day; and who has even offered to marry me, in the middle of all this madness!

I think that writing a book on color is always intimidating – there are far too many beautiful colors and combinations in the world to fit in to any book. I hope that this book will help others to appreciate our fascinating planet and to understand the joy of finding beauty in our simple everyday experiences.

Color accuracy

Unfortunately for anyone who uses color, it is always limiting when trying to reproduce real color in a printed book, due to the limited colors in printing inks. However, great length and pain has gone into achieving good color representation in this book, which can be reproduced in your home, by you. The positive outcome of this is that your final interior will definitely be much more exciting than the flat color on these pages!

It is important to remember that in printing there may be very slight alterations in the final color. Also, paint color may vary slightly from one batch to another, so always try to buy color made in the same batch.